CHILDREN'S ENCYCLOPEDIA

THE WORLD OF KNOWLEDGE

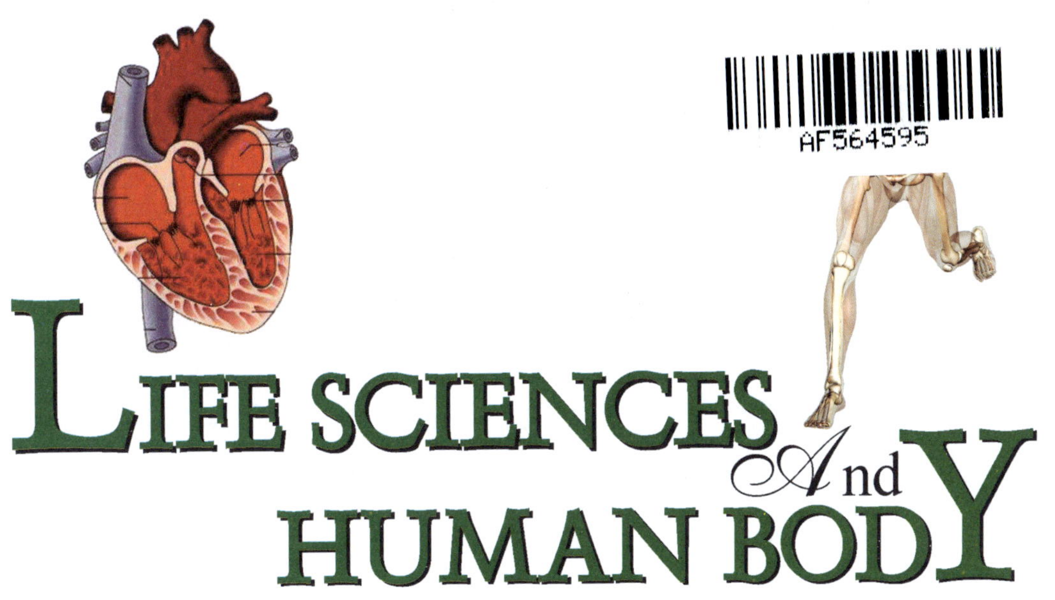

LIFE SCIENCES And HUMAN BODY

by

Manasvi Vohra

Published by:

Head Office
F-2/16, Ansari Road, Daryaganj,
New Delhi-110002 ☎ 23240026, 27, 28
✉ info@vspublishers.com
🌐 www.vspublishers.com

Regional Office
5-1-707/1, Brij Bhawan (Beside Central
Bank of India Lane) Bank Street, Koti,
Hyderabad - 500 095 ☎ 040-24737290
✉ vspublishershyd@gmail.com

Online Brandstore: amazon.in/vspublishers

Buy Books Online: amazon • Flipkart | **Follow us on:**    

ISBN 978-93-505703-6-4

New Edition

Cataloging in Publication Data--DK
Courtesy: D.K. Agencies (P) Ltd. <docinfo@dkagencies.com>

Vohra, Manasvi, author.
Life sciences and human body / by Manasvi Vohra. -- New edition.
pages cm. -- (Children's encyclopedia : the world of knowledge)
ISBN 9789350570364

1. Life sciences--Encyclopedias, Juvenile. 2. Human anatomy--Encyclopedias, Juvenile. I. Title. II. Series: Children's encyclopedia : the world of knowledge.

LCC QH307.2.V64 2024 | DDC 570.3 23

Printed at : Param Offsetters, Okhla, New Delhi–110020

PUBLISHER'S NOTE

V&S Publishers is glad to announce the launch of a unique, fully *coloured set of five books* under the head, ***Children's Science Encyclopedia – The World of Knowledge.*** The set of 5 books namely – ***Life Sciences and the Human Body***, ***Physics and Chemistry***, ***Space Science and Electronics***, ***Scientists and Inventions***, and ***General Knowledge*** has been especially developed keeping in mind the students and children of all age groups, particularly from 6 to 14 years of age. Our main aim is to arouse the interest and solve the queries of the school children regarding the various and diverse topics of Science and help them master the subject thoroughly. After the resounding success of 71 Science Trailblazing Series, we present you with this new arrival of ours.

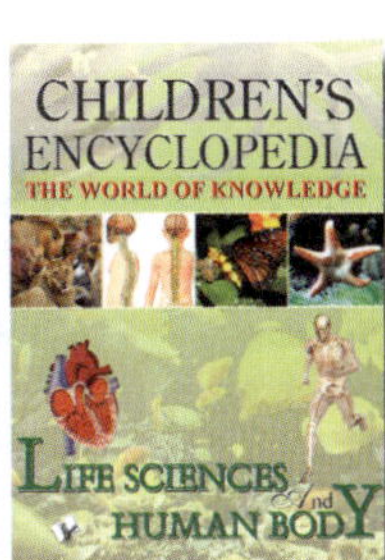

In the book, ***Life Sciences and Human Body,*** the author has broadly dealt with some interesting and fascinating Scientific facts in the first part (Part-I) like *The Atmosphere and its Composition, The Change of Seasons, Why do Plants and Animals become Extinct, The Vision of Owls, What is Milk made up of*, etc. The second part (Part-II), on the other hand, focusses mainly on the amazing and interesting facts of the 'World' such as: *The Stone Age, The Story behind the Name, 'America', How was the United Kingdom formed, What is Red Cross, The Story behind Mona Lisa*, and so on...

Each chapter is followed by a section called **Quick Facts** that contains a set of interesting and fascinating facts about the topics already discussed in the chapter. There are also **Exercises** compiled at the end of the book followed by a **Glossary** of difficult words and scientific terms to make the book complete and comprehensive.

Though our aim is to be flawless, but errors might have crept in inadvertently. So we request our esteemed readers to read the book thoroughly and offer valuable suggestions wherever necessary to improve and enhance the quality of the book. Hope it interests you all and serves its purpose well.

CONTENTS

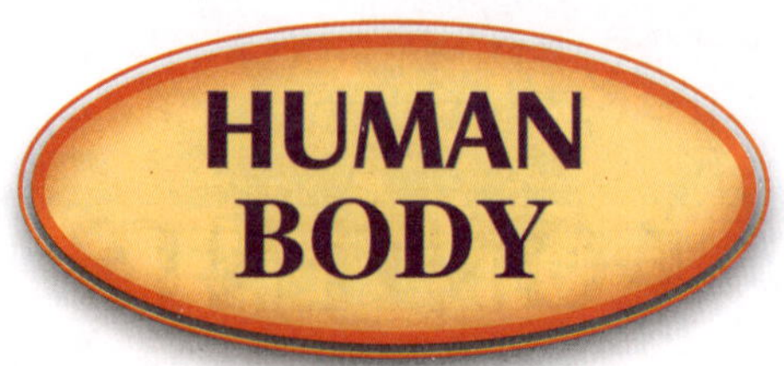

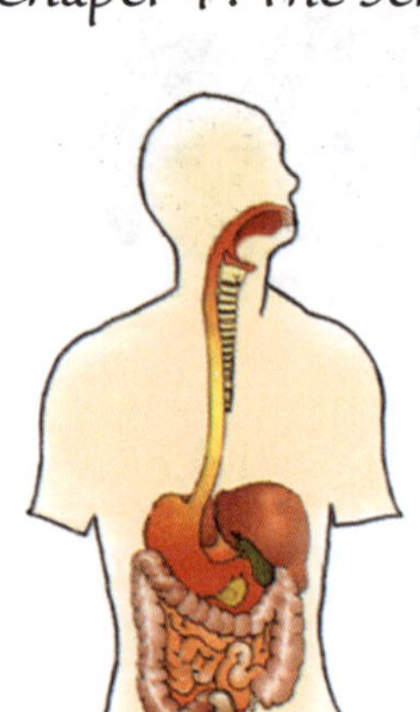

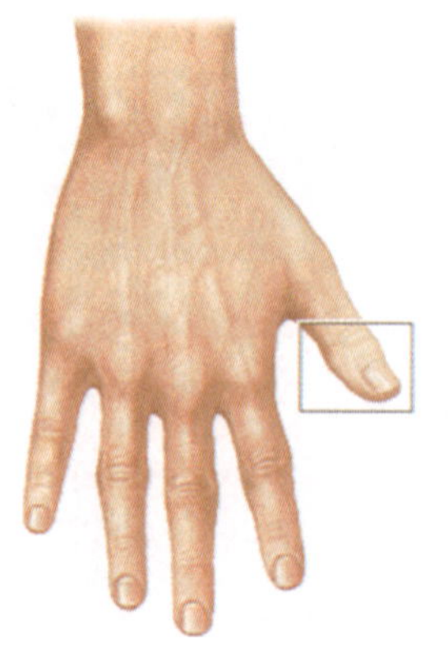

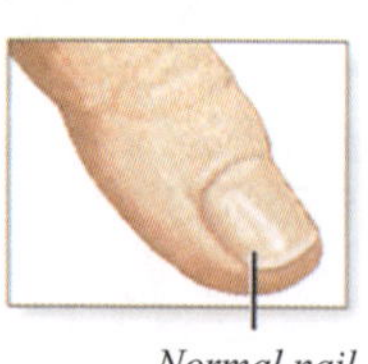

Normal nail

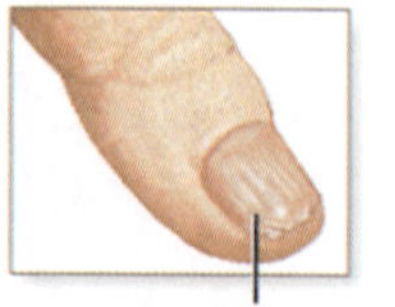

Dry, brittle nail

WHAT IS LIFE SCIENCE?

Millions of things surround us. We distinguish these things and the world around us as living and non-living based on the similarities that each of these possess. The scientific study of living beings is called *life science*.

Living beings possess special characteristics that make them different from non-living things. They are as follows:

(i) They Move

Unlike non-living things, living things can *move from one place to another* in search of food, shelter, protection against enemies, and favourable weather conditions.

Animals use their legs to move, birds and insects use their wings, fishes swim, and snakes crawl.

A Polar Bear on the Move

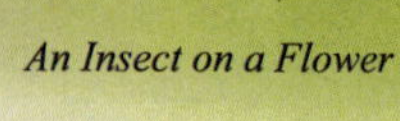

An Insect on a Flower

Bird Flying

Although plants do not move, they are considered as living things as their parts show movements. The best example of this is how a sunflower turns towards the sun, a touch-me-not closes its leaves when touched, and a poppy flower closes its petals at night and opens them in the morning.

A Snake Crawling

(ii) They Grow

Seeds Germinating

Living things grow and change their shape as they develop. Plants develop from seeds; animals grow from eggs or from a foetus.

Hatching of An Egg

(iii) They Breathe

A Human Nose

Living things breathe to remain alive. Human beings have a nose to breathe. Some insects have air holes to breathe. Fishes have gills, whereas plants have stomata to breathe.

Snakes Respire through Skin

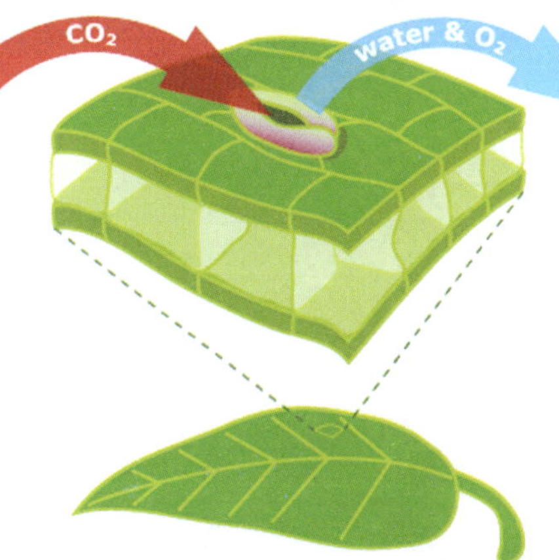

A Leaf with Stomata

(iv) They Need Food

Living things require food to grow. Plants produce their own food through the process of *photosynthesis* and animals feed on plants or other animals to survive.

Cows Grazing in the Open Field

(v) They Feel

Sunflowers Facing the Sun

Living beings have sense organs. They can feel pain, smell their food and feel the changes happening around them. Though plants do not have any sense organs, they respond to the changes in their environment, which proves that they too feel.

(vi) They Reproduce

A Young Animal with its Mother

Reproduction forms a major process in the lives of living things. They multiply. Plants produce seeds that grow into new plants. Animals give birth to young ones that help in continuing their life cycle.

(vii) They Perish

Every living being ceases to exist after some time. Age, harsh weather, climate change, diseases and natural calamities such as droughts, floods, etc., are the main reasons for destruction or death of living things.

A Withered Plant

Part - I

ANIMAL KINGDOM

Apart from the human race, there are other living things on the planet earth that make it a more beautiful place to live at. One among them is the Animal Kingdom. There are thousands of species, most of them are similar to each other, while there are others, who are completely different. They are mostly classified based on their similarities, for example – **Vertebrates** (those with a backbone) and **Invertebrates** (those without a spinal column or a backbone). Below, you will learn a lot more about different characteristics of animals, their classification, their body systems and much more.

Chapter - 1

ANATOMY

Body Systems

Several *body systems* make the body of an animal work. In most animals, (vertebrates and invertebrates), there are two major body systems:

(i) The *muscular system*

(ii) The *skeletal system*

The muscular system helps in movement of the body using muscles and the skeletal system provides structural support to the system and protects the body. These together form the **body weight**.

Apart from these, there are various other systems. These are as follows:

Digestive System

The digestive system breaks the food down to produce energy. Majority of the animals use their mouth to take in food. This process is called **ingestion**.

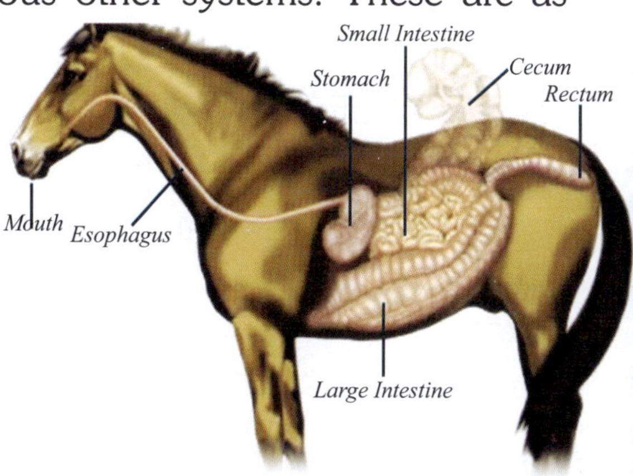

Digestive System of a Horse

Some animals like tapeworms, live in the digestive system of another animal and take in nutrients from that animal directly through their body walls.

Oysters and mussels feed on small organisms and particles from the surrounding water.

Earthworms and termites eat the dirt or wood they burrow through.

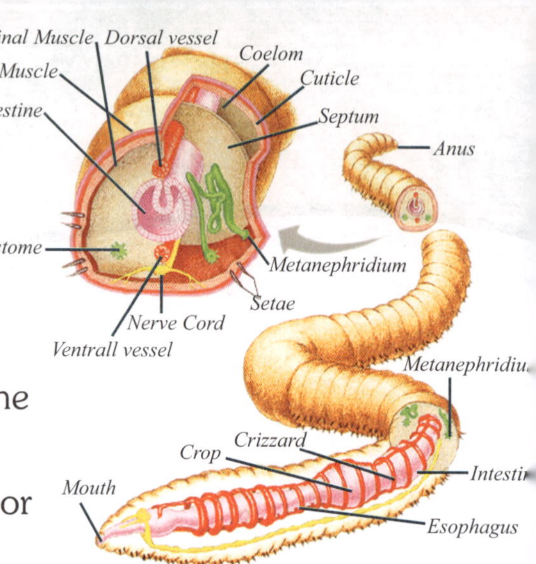

Digestive System of an Earthworm

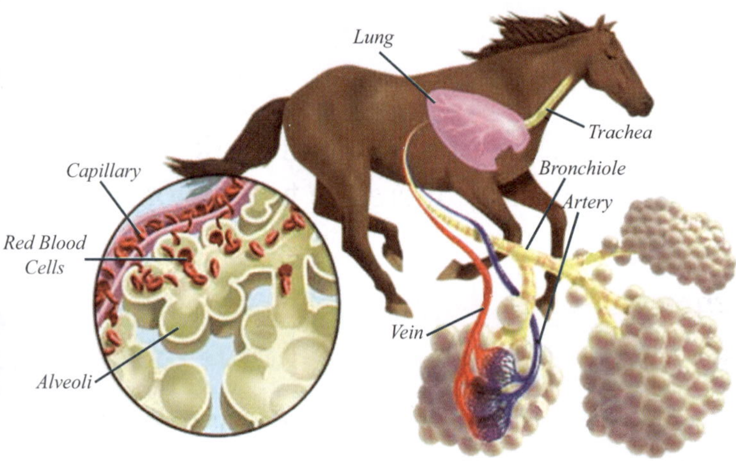

Respiratory System in a Horse

Respiratory System

The respiratory system removes carbon dioxide, which is harmful to the body, produced during the production of energy.

Simple invertebrates lack respiratory organs, whereas in amphibians, lungs and skin both serve as respiratory organs.

An elephant can breathe through its mouth as well as its trunk, so it can survive under water holding its trunk above the water level.

An Elephant Breathing through its Trunk

Circulatory System

The circulatory system circulates blood in the body, along with oxygen and carbon dioxide.

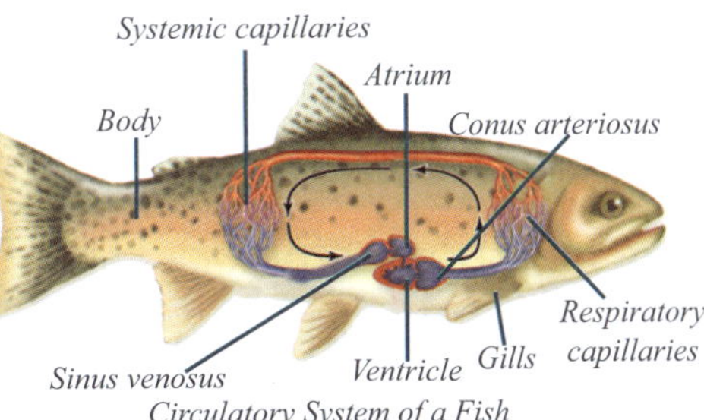

Circulatory System of a Fish

Most vertebrates have a closed cardiovascular system, which means that the blood circulates through arteries, veins and capillaries.

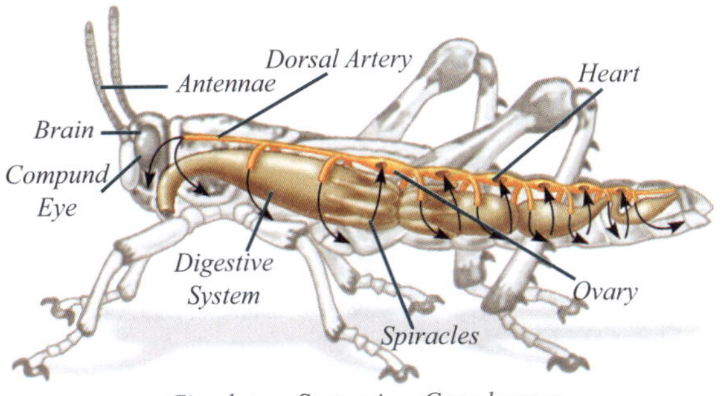

Circulatory System in a Grasshopper

Some invertebrates have an open cardiovascular system.

Excretory System

The excretory system removes the waste from the body.

Marine bony fishes suffer from a higher rate of water loss. To compensate this loss, they drink a lot of seawater. The excess salt taken in by drinking the salty seawater is removed through specialised cells in its gills.

Excretory System of Bony Fish

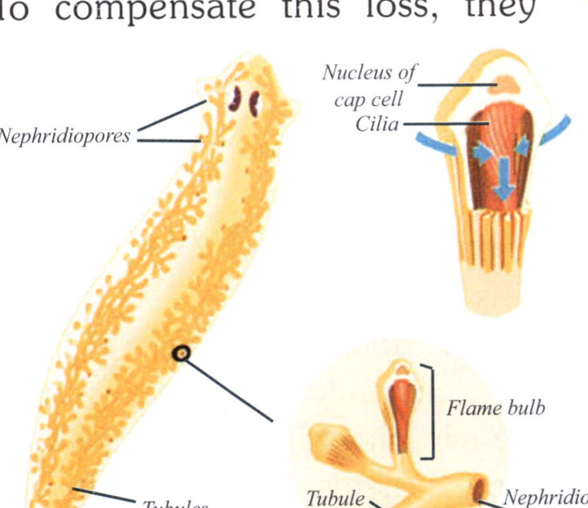

Excretory System of an Earthworm

Nervous System

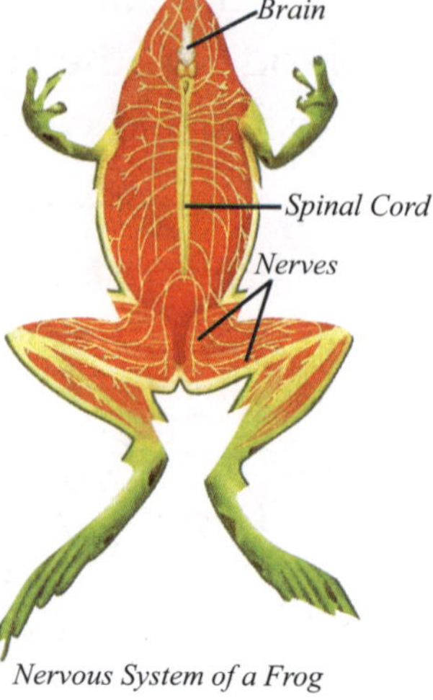

Nervous System of a Frog

The nervous system processes information and makes the body react.

The sensory organs of animals help them to react and respond to their environment. It helps them to coordinate the various systems in their bodies to attack their prey or escape from their attackers. The nervous system prompts them to escape or provide their muscles, the increased blood supply to run and attack. The respiratory system then provides the oxygen needed on account of the increased activity and once the prey is caught, the digestive system helps to digest the food.

Nervous System of a Cockroach

Endocrine System

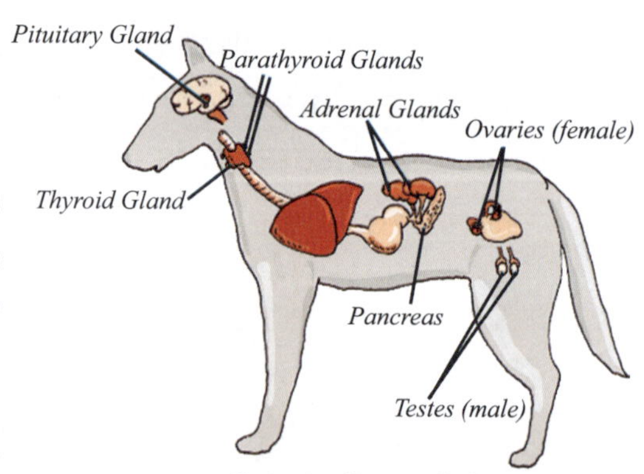

Endocrine System of a Dog

The endocrine system works with the nervous system to produce hormones or chemical substances helpful for coordination of body processes.

Mostly, animals with well-developed nervous and circulatory systems have an endocrine system. Animals have to constantly adapt to changes in the environment. The nervous and endocrine systems together help the animal to adapt to their ever-changing and new environment.

An English Bulldog

Reproductive System

The reproductive system helps to produce the young ones.

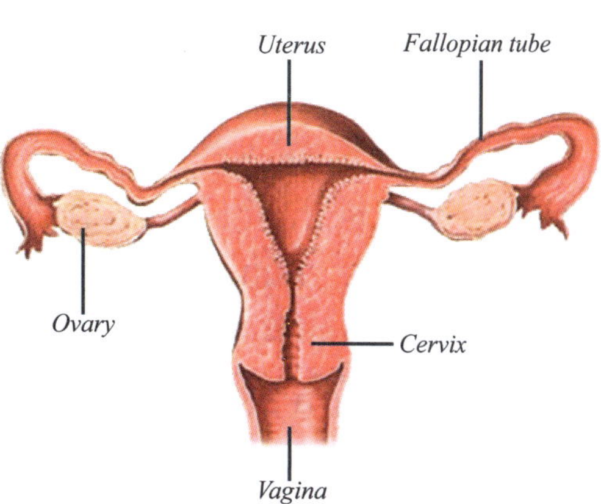

Reproductive System in Mammals

Birds, chickens and turtles lay eggs in which the young ones continue to develop. Once developed, these eggs hatch to give rise to the young ones.

A Hen Laying Eggs

Most mammals develop within the womb of the mother and are later given birth. Garter snakes and Madagascar hissing cockroaches lay eggs that hatch as soon as they are laid.

Quick Facts

- **The memory span of a goldfish is 3 seconds.**
- **A cow's sweat glands are in its nose.**
- **Lobsters have pale-blue coloured blood.**

Skeleton and Muscles

The skeleton protects the organs of the body and in some animals, it serves as an external covering.

Exoskeleton of an Arachnid (Arthropod)

The external skeleton or **exoskeleton** is usually found in invertebrates, provides them a protective covering, and guards their organs and soft tissues. Since it is difficult to grow the exoskeleton, the animals have to shed it every now and then. This external skeleton makes the body very heavy and is therefore, usually found in animals smaller in size and also in bigger animals living underwater, as the weight becomes less and manageable under water.

Endoskeleton or internal skeleton, found in most vertebrates, not only protects and gives form to the body, but also connects with the muscles, providing them the energy needed. Animals without limbs, such as earthworms and jellyfish, contract and expand their muscles to move forward, whereas those with limbs move using their muscles to push their limbs front, back, up or down.

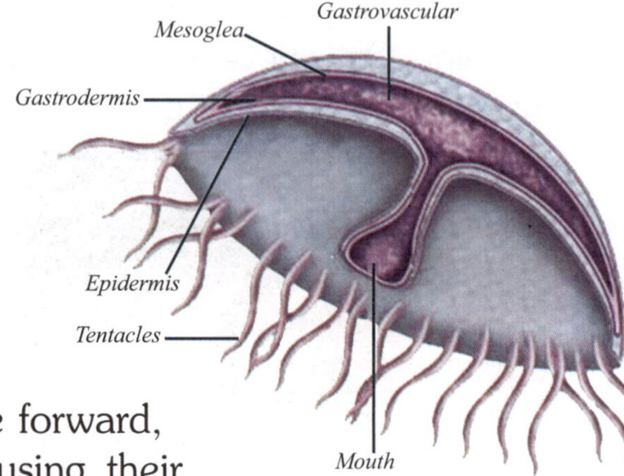

Endoskeleton of a Jellyfish

Quick Facts

- **Cats cannot move their jaws sideways.**
- **A cat has 32 muscles in each ear.**
- **A bear has 42 teeth; a mosquito has 47 teeth.**
- **A jelly fish is 95% water.**

Body Coverings

The animal body is covered with some kind of covering. In mammals, this covering is formed by the dead skin, whereas in insects, it is formed by hard proteins and water-resistant wax.

Animal with Scales (Chameleon)

Mammals have their bodies covered with extra-protective coverings in the form of scales, feathers, fur, hair and bristles. Fur and feathers help to prevent the body heat from escaping. Coloured body coverings and patterns help to provide camouflage and attract mates.

Animal with Fur (Otter)

Animals with Feathers (Cock)

Animals with Hair

Quick Facts

- **The spines of a porcupine are so light that when put in water, it floats.**
- **One can differentiate a male giraffe from a female by looking at its horns; a cow giraffe (female) has shorter horns with hair on its tips, whereas a bull giraffe (male) has longer and plain horns without hair.**
- **The red colour in the skin of a hippopotamus is a substance that protects it from sunburns.**

Senses

Senses are as useful to animals as they are to human beings. Animals need their senses to find their food and their ways. However, some animals have developed unique methods to find their ways around.

Whales, bats and dolphins are very sensitive to echolocation – they have a very strong sense of hearing that helps them navigate around and hunt for food. Though their vision is weak, they can judge their ways by sounds being reflected from the surroundings.

A Bat

Snails have eyes on two long stalks and can turn them all around to see, and flip them inside out to shut them.

Snail

Snakes can stick out their tongues and smell the air.

Cows have four times more taste buds than human beings.

Frog

Birds

Frogs can see what is behind them without turning their heads.

Birds can't move their eyes but can turn their whole heads to look around. They have twice as many bones in their necks as human beings do.

Quick Facts

- A goat has rectangular pupils.
- A scallop has 35 blue eyes.
- A chameleon's tongue is twice the length of its body.

Chapter - 2

ANIMAL CLASSIFICATION

There are millions of animals around us. With almost two million species of animals identified till date, their study becomes easier by classifying or grouping them into various categories. The classification of animals is known as **taxonomy**.

Scientists classify organisms according to their *kingdoms, phylum or phyla, classes, orders, families, genus* and *species*. While most of the animals can move; some like sea squirts spend their adult life in one place, but as young ones, they can move around freely. They can also be distinguished by their basic biological features.

Animals are broadly classified into the following two groups:

(i) Vertebrates

(ii) Invertebrates

Animals that have a backbone are called vertebrates and invertebrates include animals which do not have a backbone. Even though vertebrates are more commonly known, they are fewer in number as compared to the invertebrates. Unlike vertebrates, the invertebrates have very less features in common with each other except the lack of backbone.

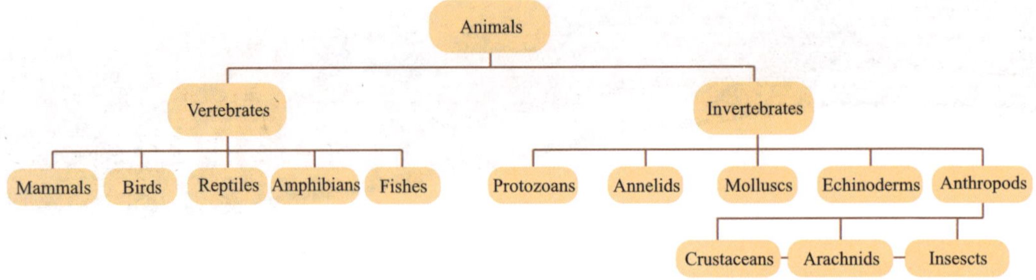

(i) Vertebrates

Vertebrates are divided into the following five main groups:

(a) Mammals

(b) Birds

(c) Reptiles

(d) Amphibians

(e) Fishes

(a) Mammals

Giraffe

Mammals are so called because they feed and nourish their young ones on the milk produced by the mother's mammary glands. They are

Cow

Monkeys

Kangaroo

mostly found on land. They adapt very easily to their surroundings, which makes them the most commonly found animal group. They have the ability to maintain their body temperatures against the changing outside weather. Some animals such as the *duck-billed platypus* and the *echidna* lay eggs even though they are mammals. On the other hand, there are mammals like *kangaroos* that give birth to the young ones like any other mammal, but they give birth at a very early stage, making their offspring undernourished. They have to carry their young ones in their pouches and nourish them with their milk.

Duck-Billed Platypus

(b) Birds

The characteristic feature of birds is their ability to fly. Their wings, feathers, and light, streamlined bodies help them fly to far-off places. However, there are birds such as the *ostriches* that cannot fly. These warm-blooded animals reproduce by laying eggs. They are known to be brilliant architects. A *weaver bird* uses grass, twigs and leaves to weave its nest using its beak. It creates an opening at the bottom of the nest to enter into its home. *Tailor birds* too make their

A Bird Flying

An Ostrich is a Flightless Bird

A Weaver Bird Weaving its Nest

nests by sewing large leaves using cotton thread and its beak as a needle. At the same time, there are birds like the cuckoo that does not build its own nest and lays its eggs in the nests of other birds.

A Tailor Bird and its Nest

(c) Reptiles

Snakes, lizards, crocodiles, alligators, tortoises and turtles form the group of animals called the *reptiles*. These are *egg-laying animals*. They live mainly in water and lay their eggs on land. They are *cold-blooded vertebrates* that have a tough skin covered with scales.

Crocodile

Lizard

Tortoise

(d) Amphibians

Amphibians are classified as animals that live both on land as well as in water. Newts, salamanders, frogs and toads are some of these cold-blooded vertebrates. They start as larvae under water, breathing through gills, and as adults, live on land and take in oxygen through lungs. (Their body temperatures change according to the outside temperatures.

Salamander

Frog

(e) Fishes

Gills of a Fish

Fishes are known to be the *first backboned animals* to appear on the earth. A typical fish breathes or respires through gills, has a body covered with scales, moves using fins, and is a cold-blooded vertebrate. They are either freshwater bound or inhabitants of the sea. However, there are a few species that switch between the two environments.

Shark

Quick Facts

- **A housefly can live for only 14 days.**
- **The octopus has three hearts.**
- **A starfish is the only animal that can turn its stomach inside out.**

(ii) Invertebrates

The invertebrates are divided into five major groups:

(a) Protozoans

(b) Annelids

(c) Molluscs

(d) Echinoderms

(e) Arthropods

Arthropods can be further divided into the following three groups:

- Crustaceans
- Arachnids
- Insects

(a) Protozoans

Protozoans are single-celled animals that are so small that they can only be seen under a microscope. They have the ability to move and reproduce like any multi-cellular animal.

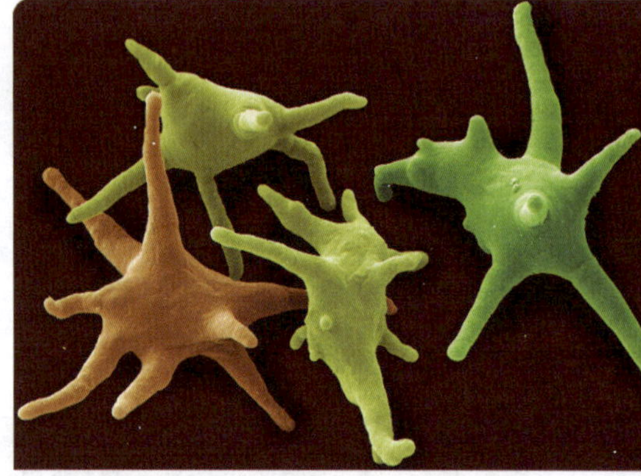

Amoeba

Amoeba and *flagellates* are types of protozoa. They form a vital link of the food chain. They feed on algae and bacteria by either absorbing them through their cell membranes or by consuming them through their mouth-like openings. Then they themselves become the food for fishes and other animals. They have stomach-like structures called *vacuoles* to digest their food.

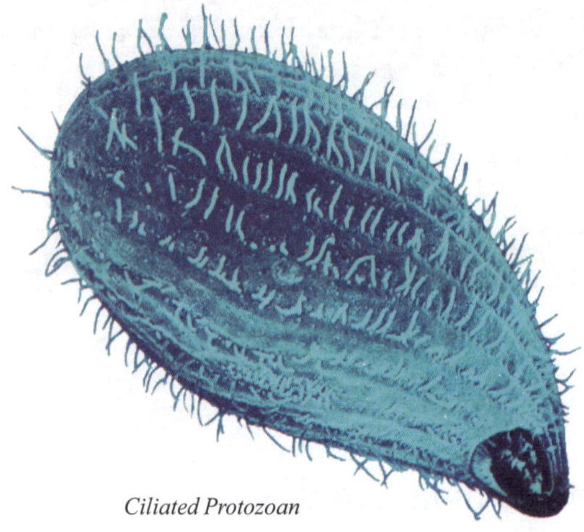

Ciliated Protozoan

They even respire or breathe through their cell membranes and reproduce by splitting their bodies into half.

(b) Annelids

Worm

Leech

Thousands of species of annelids have been discovered till date. These include some known *worms* and *leeches*. Their sizes range from a few inches to a hundred feet. Their bodies are divided into *segments* and have well-developed internal organs. They have *no limbs*.

(c) Molluscs

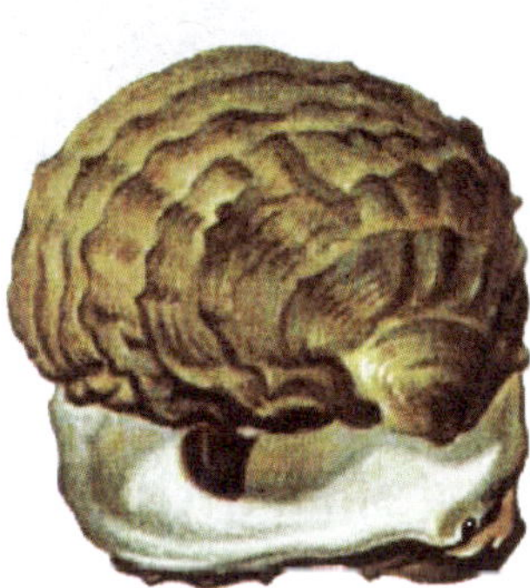

Oyster

Fossils over millions of years old have proven that molluscs were one of the *first organisms on the Earth*. They have soft bodies covered with hard shells. Some molluscs, such as *snails* and *slugs* can be found on land, whereas molluscs, such as *oysters*, *mussels*, *clams*, *squids* and *octopuses* are found under water. Molluscs living on land have flat soles, which help them move, whereas those living in water move forward by pumping out water using their bodies.

Octopus

Squid

(d) Echinoderms

Sea Cucumber

Marine animals that live in the ocean are called echinoderms. *Starfish*, *sea urchin*, *sand dollar*, and *sea cucumber* are some well-known echinoderms. The central part of their body contains the spine, mouth and other organs.

Starfish

(e) Arthropods

Crustaceans

Crustaceans are mostly found in the oceans or other water bodies. The most commonly known crustaceans are *crabs*, *lobsters* and *barnacles*. Their bodies are covered by hard, external shells, which protect their bodies. Their heads have antennae which form a part of their sensory system. Their legs help them crawl and swim. Many crustaceans have claws that help them crawl or eat.

Lobster

Crab

Arachnids

Spiders, *scorpions*, *ticks* and *mites* are some commonly known arachnids. They too have a hard

Scorpion

Spider

external skeleton. Most arachnids like spiders have eight legs that help them to walk. Most spiders have eight eyes and fangs that can inject poison into their prey. Scorpions are also arachnids, and also have eight legs, and a pair of pincers for catching and holding their prey. However, they use their tails to sting their enemies. *Mites* and *ticks* are small, parasitic arachnids that live on the blood and tissue fluid of other animals and can occasionally transmit diseases.

Insects

Insects form the largest group of arthropods. They include fly, mosquito, beetle, butterfly, moth, dragonfly and bee. Insects have a hard external skeleton that covers their bodies. This makes it difficult for their cover to grow as they grow. Hence, they have to shed their exoskeleton regularly. The head of the insect has a pair of antennae and compound eyes, which means they have many lenses for each eye, for good eyesight. They may also have wings.

Dragonfly

Fly

Moth

Quick Facts

- The largest frog in the world is the Goliath frog.
- A woodpecker can peck 20 times per second.
- The smallest mammal in the world is the bumblebee bat found in Thailand. It weighs less than a penny.
- Vertebrates are further divided into the following five main groups:
  - Mammals: Monkeys, Human Beings, Bats, Cows, Dogs
  - Birds: Tailor Bird, Weaver Bird, Ostrich, etc.
  - Reptiles: Snakes, Lizards, Tortoises and many more.
  - Amphibians: Frogs, Salamanders
  - There are more species of fish than all the species of amphibians, reptiles, birds and mammals.
  - The largest fish is the great whale shark which can reach upto 50 feet in length, and the smallest fish is the Philippine goby that is less than 1/3 of an inch when fully grown.
  - Prawns and sharks are also grouped under fishes.

Chapter - 3

ANIMAL BEHAVIOUR

Habitat

A habitat is the place where an animal lives. A habitat, in ecological terms is called a **biome**. It provides the animal with food, water and shelter, i.e., almost everything, it needs to survive. Based on the habitat where they live, animals can be classified as:

- *Terrestrial*
- *Aquatic*
- *Arboreal*
- *Amphibians*
- *Aerial*

Terrestrial animals live primarily on the ground, unlike *arboreal* animals that live on trees or *aerial* animals that are airborne. Aquatic animals live in water, whereas amphibians live both on land as well as in water. However, this classification can be often confusing. There are many animals, such as penguins and seals, which live on land and derive their food from water, and yet are classified as terrestrial animals. Also, there are many animals that spend half of their life cycle in water, such as frogs. They give birth and grow in water and spend their adult life on land.

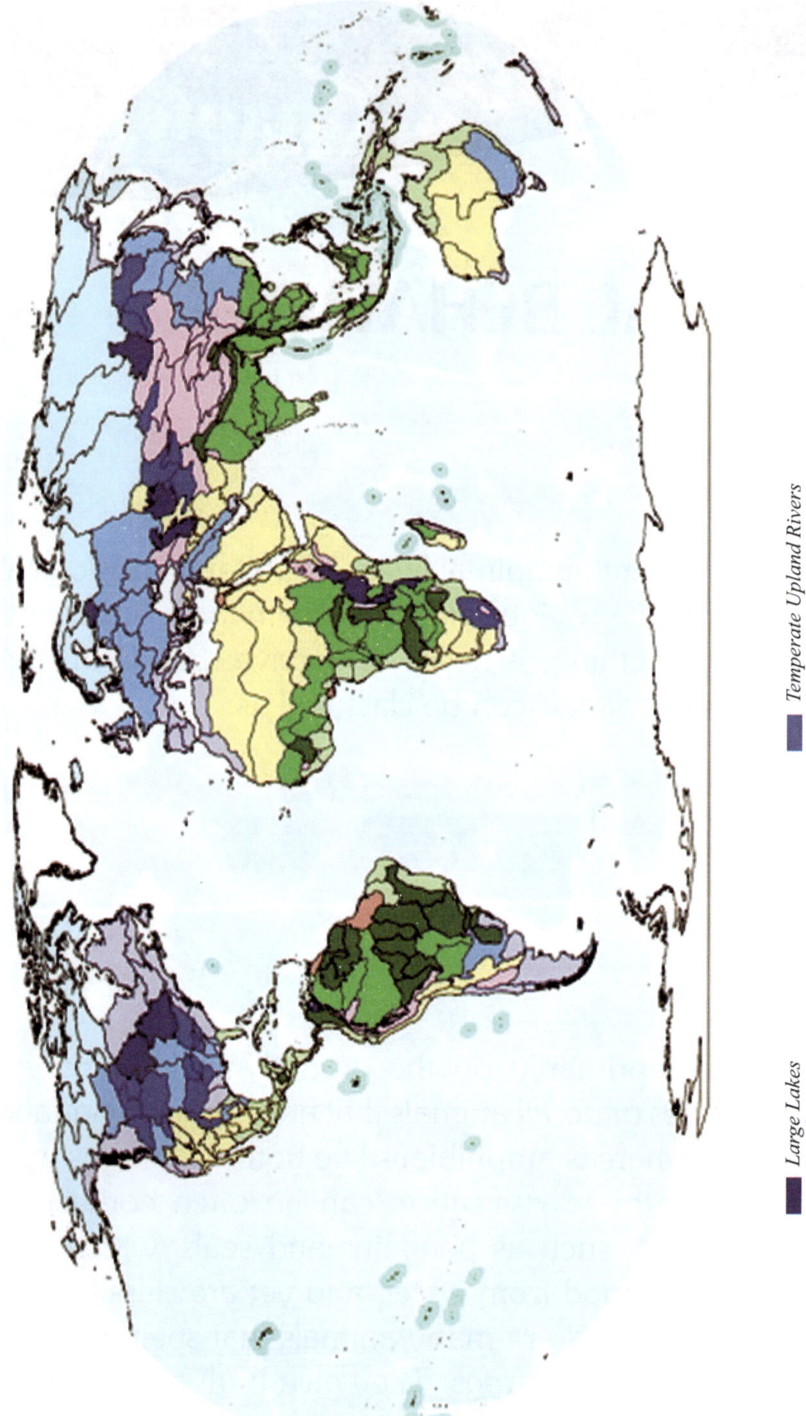

Large Lakes
Large River Deltas
Polar Freshwaters
Montane Freshwaters
Temperate Coastal Rivers
Temperate Floodplain Rivers and Wetlands
Temperate Upland Rivers
Tropical and Subtropical Coastal Rivers
Tropical and Subtropical Floodplain Rivers and Wetlands
Tropical and Subtropical Upland Rivers
Xeric Freshwater and Endorheic Basins
Oceanic Islands

Adapting to the Habitat

Some animals are capable of adapting to different environments and climates, yet they are mostly bound to one habitat. Grasslands serve as a major habitat for many animals. These regions receive

Desert Animals in their Natural Habitat

more rainfall than the deserts, making them not too dry, and less rainfall than the rainforests, making them not wet enough for dense vegetation. Grasslands are mainly covered by tall or short grass and non-woody plants, but sometimes by woody plants, trees and shrubs. They are favourable for the animals whose lives depend upon grazing as the animals can digest the grass well. The roots of these plant serve as a potential source of food for many animals and insects living in this habitat. The root system also holds the soil together, reducing the

Grassland Animals in their Natural Habitat

chances of it caving in, and thus, providing burrowing animals with a home. However, grasslands make it difficult for animals to hide, exposing them to predators and increasing the risk of being attacked. Also, it is dangerous for the young ones, who are at greater risks of being attacked or trampled under the feet of the animals grazing on land. Other such habitats are formed by deserts, forests, mountains, Polar regions, rivers and wetlands, coral reefs and urban areas.

Homes

Animals build their homes or use the existing, natural or man-made homes to live. However, their purpose of choosing a home may differ. Rock caves, for instance, are used by several animals for varied reasons depending on their habitats or habits. They protect the tigers from heat, provide shelter to brown bears living in the mountainous regions, help certain animals

Hives

Burrows

Nests

Caves

Tree homes

(Moray eels) to hide and attack their prey, and protect a bat from the daylight. Other types of homes for animals are burrows, tree homes, hives, nests, etc.

Effects of Change

Animals learn to adapt to the changing times and climate. However, an animal cannot adapt very quickly in an alien habitat and would hence, cease to survive. The environmental and climatic changes, taken place over the years, affecting the habitats, have thus led to the extinction of many species of animals and are still pushing many to the verge of extinction.

Migration

Migration is the seasonal or annual journey of animals in search of better living conditions. It could be because of the availability of food, seasonal change, mating opportunities, etc. Some animals, such as the White-throated Dipper, which changes the altitudinal levels to escape the cold, migrate to shorter distances, whereas many animals, such as the Arctic terns, which travel between Poles, cover greater distances. After staying in the new habitat for a short while, the migratory animals return to their original habitat. The Canada geese, for instance, travel to the Arctic Circle in the spring and return to warmer places in the south during autumn. However, a Monarch butterfly never completes its migratory cycle on its own. It reproduces on its journey and then the journey is carried on by its next generations.

Monarch Butterfly

Artic Terns

Quick Facts

- **Antarctica is the only continent that does not have reptiles or snakes.**
- **Penguins live to the south of the equator.**
- **Apart from the few protected ones in the national parks of Gir, India, and other such artificial or man-made environments, lions are now naturally found only in Africa.**

HUNTING AND FEEDING

Food habits

Animals obtain energy from food. Those animals that survive by feeding on other animals, either as *predators* or as *scavengers*, are called **carnivorous**.

Carnivorous

Predators hunt and kill other animals for food, while **scavengers** feed on the carcass or body of already dead animals. The characteristic features of predators, such as sharp teeth and claws, make it possible for them to hunt for

Herbivores

Omnivorous

Scavengers

Parasites

food. Carnivorous animals, such as tigers, lions, crocodiles, snakes and frogs are predators, whereas vultures, spotted hyenas, flesh flies, and coyotes are scavengers. The animals that feed on plant matter are **herbivores**. Most domestic animals like cows, buffaloes, donkeys, etc. are herbivorous animals. However, there are some animals that feed on both plants and animals. Such animals are called **omnivorous**. There are also animals that feed on other living organisms. They are called **parasites**.

Defence Mechanisms

It is the basic nature of every living being to develop defence mechanisms to protect themselves from danger. Escaping the threat by using their speed, spitting venom, using their bright coloured bodies to distract their attackers, or going into hiding are some of the defence mechanisms used by animals. The other method is camouflage, where an animal changes its their colour to blend itself with the colour of its environment. Chameleons and octopuses have the ability to change colour to merge with their surroundings, making them invisible to their predators. A herd of zebras moving together can form a brilliant camouflage, as their stripes together look like a giant mass of black and white stripes, making it difficult for the predator to spot an individual zebra. A puffer fish inflates its body, making pointed spines stick out, and thus, it becomes difficult to attack it.

Chameleon

Herd of Zebras

A Puffer Fish

Quick Facts

- **A poison arrow frog has so much poison that it can harm about 2200 people in one squirt.**
- **No two zebras have exactly the same stripes.**
- **Dolphins do not drink the water of the sea in which they live, but acquire water from feeding on water-rich food, such as sea cucumbers and squids.**
- **Tigers have retractable claws, which means they can take in and bring out their claws when needed.**

Birth and Development

Reproduction forms an important process in the life of any living being. It helps the species to multiply and evolve. Animals reproduce in the following two ways:

(i) Asexually

(ii) Sexually

In asexual reproduction, an animal does not require a partner. It divides its own body to give birth to a young one. The biggest disadvantage of this method is that the newly formed animal is exactly like its parent, making them vulnerable to all the dangers and diseases that the parent faces.

In sexual reproduction, an animal usually finds another animal of its kind, usually of the opposite gender, and they together produce a young one that has the qualities of both the parents. This induces variety in the species, but makes it difficult for the mother, as she is the only one who has to give birth to the baby. Some animals

Animals with their Young Ones

lay eggs that hatch into young ones, whereas some directly give birth to younger animals. In such cases, the newborns are generally undernourished and are fed on the milk of their mothers.

Quick Facts

- If the eggs are incubated at over 33°C, then the egg hatches into a male or 'bull' crocodile. At lower temperatures, only female or 'cow' crocodiles develop.
- Pandas, when born are as tiny as rats but, grow fully when they reach the age of four.
- A male penguin warms the egg laid by the female penguin without eating or feeding, and in the process loses 40 percent of its weight.

Whale

Glow Worm with its Tail Light on

Communication

All animals communicate to their own kind in different ways. Apart from the most common ways of communication, such as facial expression and eye contact, animals use some specific ways, such as light, sound, and even scent as a means of communication. Glow worms, for instance, turn their light on to attract their potential mates. Many animals use sound to communicate, such as from small creatures like crickets to large ones, such as whales. Animals that get separated from their herd in the grassland find their way back by smelling the scent trails left by the hoofs of those in the herd. However, these methods of communication can often draw the enemies closer and thus, prove to be a disadvantage.

Quick Facts

- **Giraffes have no vocal chords and cats have 100 vocal chords.**
- **An injured or sick dolphin's cries can make other dolphins arrive to help raise it to the surface of the water so that it becomes easy for the dolphin to breathe.**
- **Blue and fin whales can make the loudest sound that any animal can make.**

Part - II

PLANT KINGDOM

Just like the Animal Kingdom, the Plant Kingdom too forms a part of the living creatures on our planet, earth. Scientists have traced the origin of the plant kingdom to algae in freshwater. Today, we have around **300, 000 species of plants** that adorn our planet. Plants give us **oxygen** and they also provide **food** to humans and animals. Similar to the Animal Kingdom, plants also reproduce and are classified based on their similarities, for example, **Terrestrial plants** (plants that grow on land) and **Aquatic plants** (plants that grow in water).

To find more interesting details about the Plant Kingdom go throug the following chapters.

Chapter - 1

PARTS OF A PLANT

A plant can be divided into the following two main parts:

(i) Root

(ii) Shoot

Leaf

Shoot/Stem

Roots

Parts of a Plant

(i) Root

The root is the part of plant under the ground. It holds the plant firmly to the ground, absorbs water and minerals from the soil, and sends it to different parts of the plant. Some roots like radish and carrots store food in them.

There are two different types of roots:

- *Tap root*
- *Fibrous root*

Tap root: Tap root has one main root, broad on the part attached to the plant and narrower at the other. It has many small roots growing on its side. Plants like mustard, radish and beans have a tap root system.

A Tap Root

Fibrous root: Fibrous roots look like a bunch of many thin roots. Rice, wheat and onions have a fibrous root system.

Fibrous Roots

(ii) Shoot

The shoot includes all the parts of a plant above the ground. This includes stems, branches, leaves, flowers and fruits.

Stem: Different plants have different kinds of stems, from weak to thick and hard stems. Climbers like money plant have extremely weak stems that need support. They cling on to other plants and buildings for support. Potato, onion and ginger have stems below the soil and they store food in them. Stems support the plant, take the water from the roots and distribute it to different parts of the plant, thus help in the process of food production.

Leaves: Leaves prepare food for the plant using air, water and sunlight. The tiny veins in the leaf allow the water to get to the parts of the leaves. On the reverse side of the leaf, there are small pores called the **stomata**, through which carbon dioxide gets in and

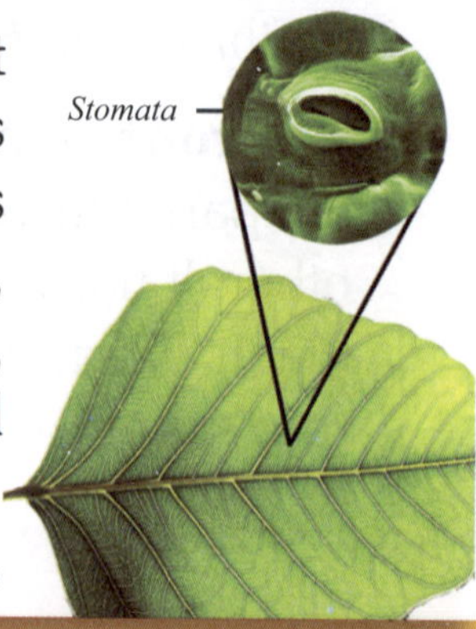

A Leaf Showing the Stomata

the oxygen escapes. Cabbages have leaves that store food.

A Flower – The Reproductive Organ of a Plant

Flowers: In many flowering plants, the flowers form the reproductive organs that contain pollen grains that help the plant to produce fruits. Some plants, such as cucumber, melons and pumpkins have flowers with either only the male parts or the female parts, whereas, others, such as rose and hibiscus have both male and female parts in the same flower.

A flower can be divided into the following parts:

Male Parts

Stamen: The anther and filament together form the stamen. It produces pollen. The number of stamens and petals are usually the same in a flower.

Connective
Anther
Microsporangium

Male Parts of a Plant (Stamen)

- **Anther:** This part of the stamen produces and contains the pollen. It is usually on top of a long, hair-like stalk.
- **Filament:** This is the thin stalk on top of which the anther sits.

Female Parts

Pistil: It includes the stigma, style and ovary.

- **Stigma:** It is the bulblike, sticky structure of the plant on which the pollen grains stick.
- **Style:** It is the long, stalk-like structure on which

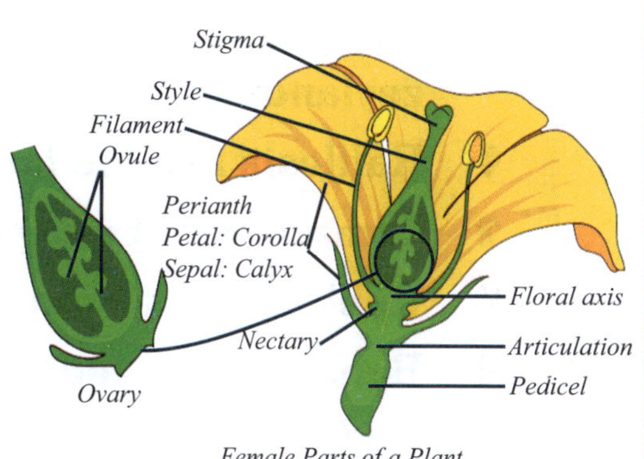

Female Parts of a Plant

the stigma rests. It separates the stigma and the ovary to avoid contamination of pollen.

- **Ovary:** This is the seed-containing part at the bottom of the flower. These seeds turn into fruits. The ovary contains ovules.
- **Ovule:** It is the part of the ovary that turns into seeds.

Other Parts

- **Petal:** These are the colourful and bright parts of the flowers that attract bees and butterflies.
- **Sepal:** The green leaf-like structure that covers the outside of a flower bud, protecting it before it opens and blooms into a flower.

Litchi

- **Fruits:** Fruits form a covering for the seeds. The seed remains protected inside the fruit and helps in producing new plants.

Quick Facts

- **Saffron used in food items is the dried stigmas of the saffron flower.**
- **Cinnamon is the bark of the Cinnamomum zeylandicum tree rolled up.**
- **Rafflesia has the largest known flower in the world.**
- **Tomato is not a vegetable but the fruit of a plant.**
- **Cabbage and Spinach are leafy vegetables.**
- **Banana is a seedless fruit.**

Chapter - 2

PHOTOSYNTHESIS

Every living being requires food. Human beings cook their own food, animals hunt for food or feed on plants, and plants make their own food. The process of food preparation in plants is called **photosynthesis**.

The Process

Leaves of plants serve as a *kitchen*, where the food is prepared. The preparation of food in plants requires the following three things:

(i) Carbon dioxide

(ii) Sunlight

(iii) Water

Different parts of a plant help to get these required ingredients to the leaf. Leaves contain a chemical called **chlorophyll**. This chemical absorbs **sunlight** from the environment and converts it into **chemical energy** that can be used by the plant. On the reverse side of the leaf, there are tiny pores called **stomata**. This helps to get carbon dioxide to the leaves. The roots of plant get deep into the soil and absorb water and minerals from it. The stem draws the water from the roots and distributes it to all parts of the plant.

The leaves have small **veins** that help water and other minerals to reach all the parts of a leaf. Using the water and carbon dioxide supplied by the roots, stem and the stomata respectively, and using the sunlight, the leaves prepare the food for plant. This food is then distributed by the stem and the veins to all the parts of the plant.

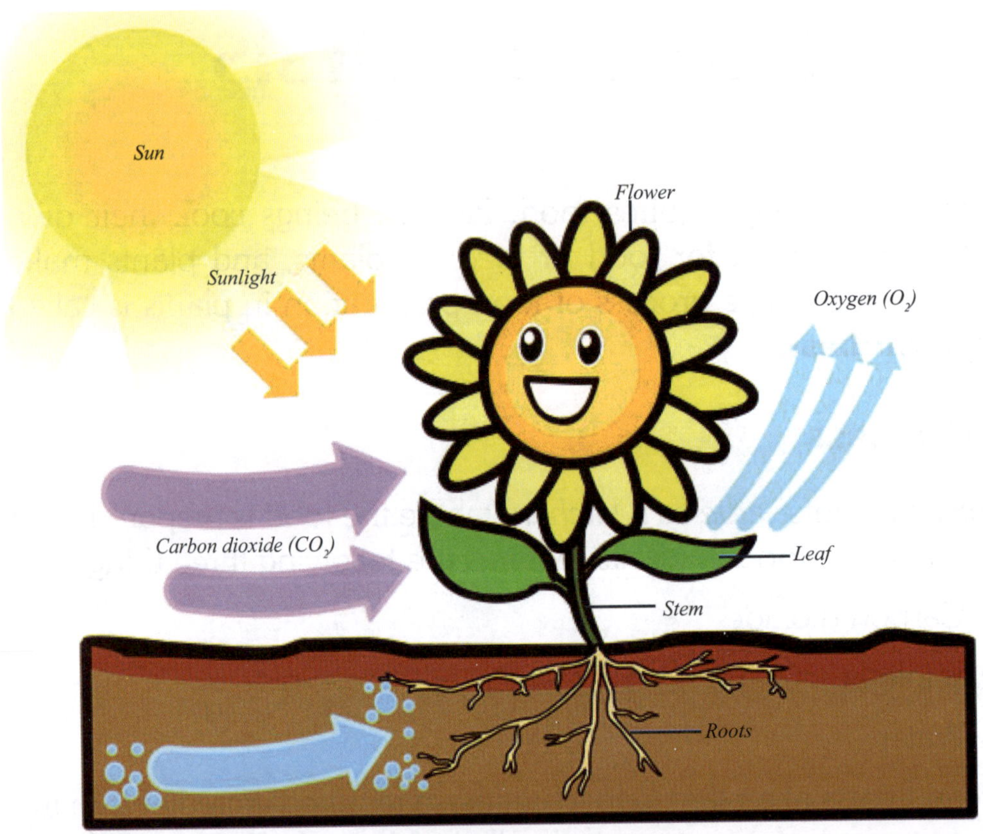

The food produced helps in the growth and development of *branches*, *leaves*, *flowers* and *fruits*. Excess food is converted into *starch* and is stored in various parts of the plant. All the plants that are able to produce food and contain chlorophyll are called Autotrophs.

Chlorophyll-lacking plants

Bracket Mushrooms

Due to the presence of chlorophyll, most plants can produce their own food. However, there are some plants, such as **fungi** that do not have chlorophyll. They have to depend on other things for their food. For instance, mushrooms, which are a type of fungi, absorb food from the soil in which they grow and bracket mushrooms that grow on trees get their food from the trees. The plants that do not contain green pigments or chlorophyll are called **Heterotrophs**.

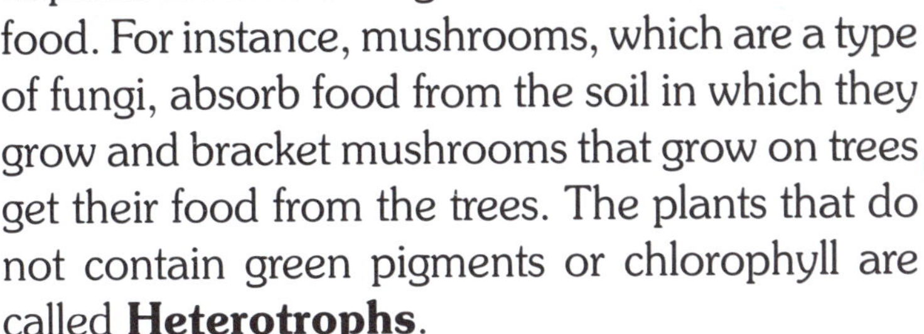

Mushrooms

Quick Facts

- **Every living being requires food.**
- **The process of food preparation in green plants with the help of water, carbon dioxide and sunlight is called photosynthesis.**
- **Leaves contain a chemical called chlorophyll that help in photosynthesis.**
- **Due to the presence of chlorophyll, most plants can produce their own food.**

GROWTH AND DEVELOPMENT

The Seed

Life of a plant begins with a seed. A tiny, lifeless-looking seed can give rise to a plant. Seeds are of the following two types:

(i) Monocotyledons

(ii) Dicotyledons

Seed Coat
Embryo
Stored Food
Monocot
Dicot

A Monocot and Dicot Seed

Monocotyledons or **Monocots** are called so as they contain one cotyledon (seed leaf), whereas, **Dicotyledons** or **Dicots** have two seed leaves. The parts of a seed are as follows:

- The seed coat is known as **testa**.
- The young root is called a **radicle**.
- The young shoot is called **plumule** and can be divided into the following two parts:
  - Hypocotyl
  - Epicotyl

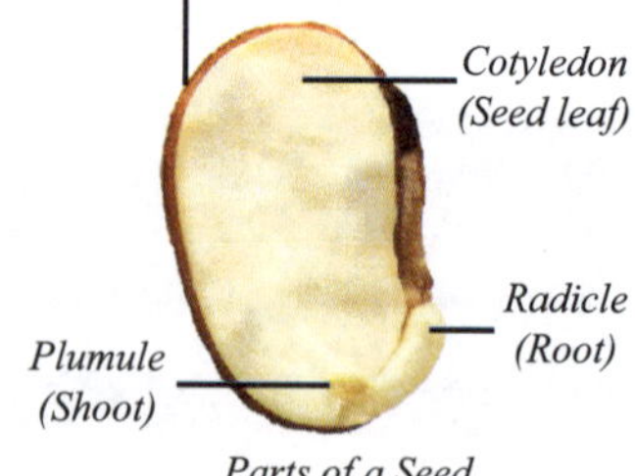

Parts of a Seed

Hypocotyl is the part of the plumule attached to the radicle, whereas, **epicotyl** forms the part of the plumule that is attached to the hypocotyl.

Cotyledon or seed leaf is a part of the seed that stores food for the embryo.

Monocots have one cotyledon and dicots have two cotyledons.

The **Endosperm** serves as a food storage in monocots.

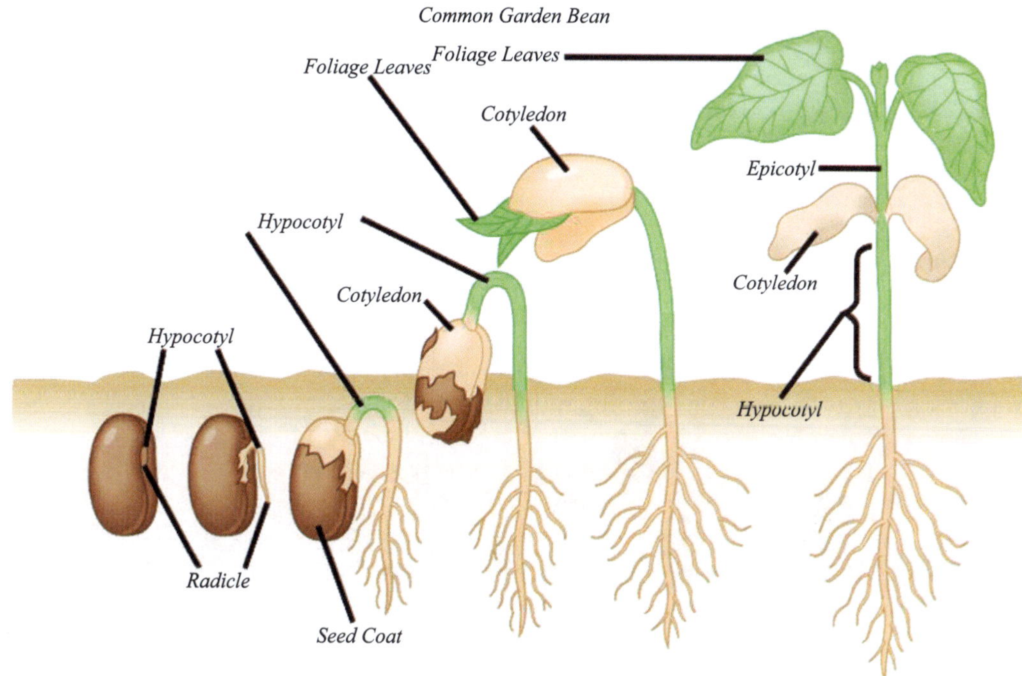

The Process of Germination

Germination

The process of formation of a plant from a seed is called germination. The whole process is divided into stages as explained diagrammatically.

Germination in Dicots

During the germination process of dicots, when the seed is buried in the soil, the primary root bursts opens the seed coat. The hypocotyl emerges from the seed coat through the soil forming an **arch**. The **epicotyl** is protected by two cotyledons. When the hypocotyl emerges out of the soil completely, it is straightened by the sunlight. The two cotyledons spread apart exposing the epicotyl, containing two primary leaves. In many dicots, cotyledons act as food storing structures. As the plant grows, the cotyledons fall apart.

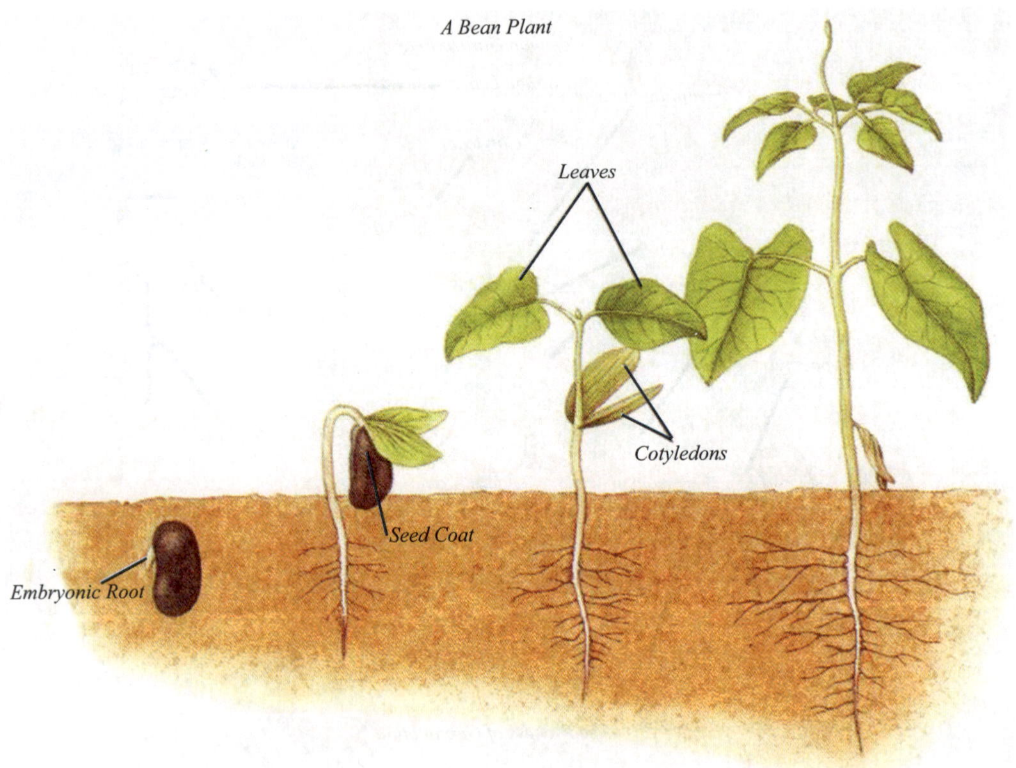

Germination in Dicots

Germination in Monocots

In monocots, the embryo of the plant rests in the seed and the starch produced during photosynthesis gets stored in the **endosperm**. A seed shows its first signs of germination when it absorbs the water and the radicle (young primary root) bursts open the testa (seed coat). The starch stored in the seed gets converted into sugar, the embryo gets enlarged, and the seed coat bursts open. The primary root develops, giving rise to the secondary roots. The *plumule* (young stem) emerges, producing its *first leaves*.

A Maze Plant

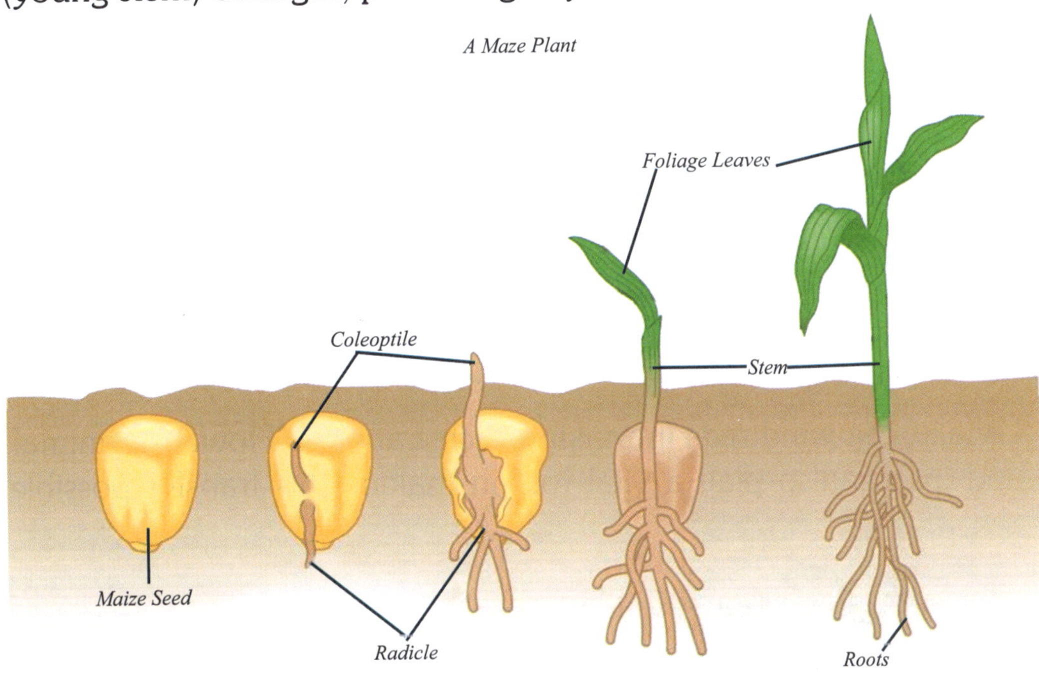

Germination in Monocots

Pollination

A very important process in the growth and development of a plant, besides germination, is pollination. It helps the plants to develop into new ones.

Pollination starts in the flower itself. The stamen of the flower produces a sticky powder called **pollen**. When this pollen is transferred to the stigma of the flower, **pollination** takes place. If the pollen from the **stamen** of a flower is transferred to the **stigma** of the same flower, it is called **self-pollination**, but if it is transferred to the stigma of another flower, it is called **cross-pollination**. Such a transfer can happen in many ways.

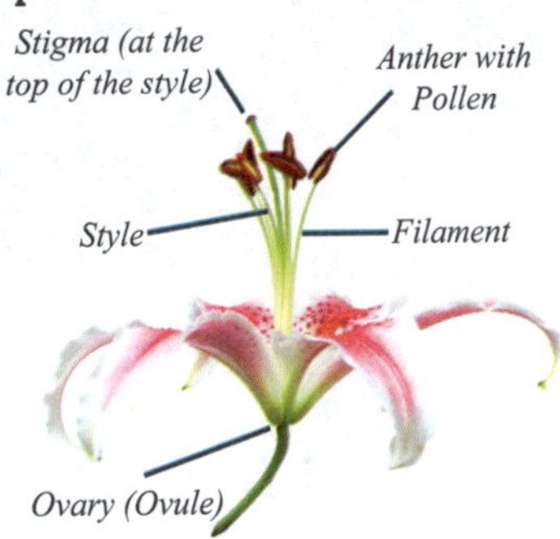

Pollination in Plants

Cross-Pollination in Plants

Usually, the wind aids in making such transfers. However, animals and insects also play a vital role in making this transfer possible.

Animals Feeding on Plants

Bees, moths, butterflies and hummingbirds are attracted by the bright colour of the flowers and when they sit on the flower to suck the nectar, the pollen gets stuck on their feet. When they move on to another flower in search of nectar, the pollen gets transferred from their feet to the stigma of another flower, resulting in pollination. Similarly, when animals come to feed on plants, the pollens get stuck to their bodies and as they move on to different pastures for food, the pollen gets rubbed off their bodies and pollinates other plants.

Fertilisation

After pollination takes place, the next step is the formation of **seeds**. This process is called fertilisation, which takes place in the **ovary**. The transfer of the pollen from the male part of the flower to the female part of the flower that takes place during the process of pollination leads to the formation of *seeds in the ovary*. With time, the ovary grows into a **fruit**, containing seeds. Once the fruits are **ripe**, they fall on the ground and help in the production of new plants. Thus, the lifecycle of a plant continues.

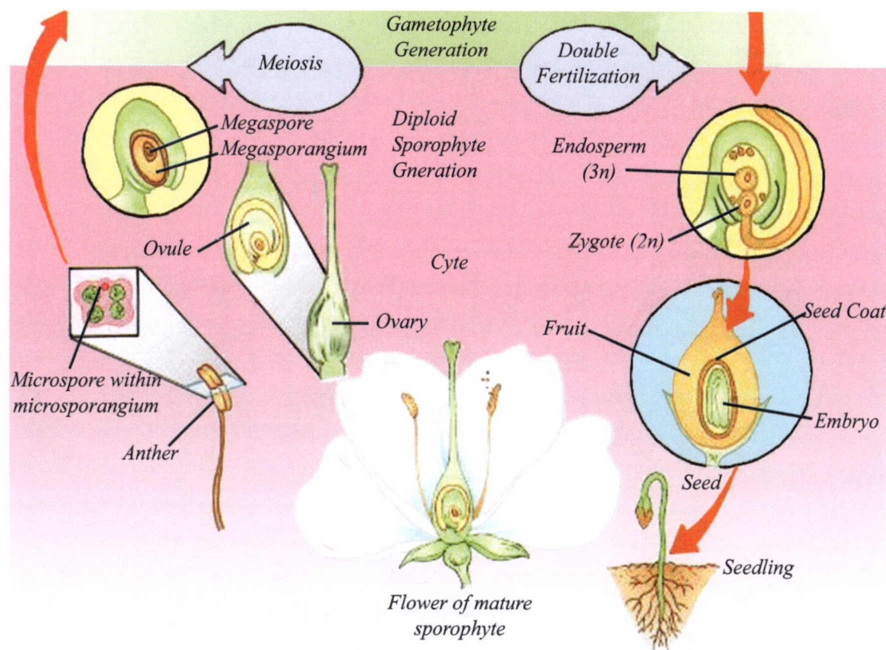

Fertilisation and Growth of a Plant

Quick Facts

- The largest seed is of the double coconut palm.
- Orchids have the tiniest seeds.
- Kiwi fruits contain up to 1000 edible seeds in it.
- Kalanchoe, a type of plant, can grow simply by placing a leaf in the soil.
- The female holly plant do not produce red berries unless there is a male holly nearby to provide the pollen.

Chapter - 4

PLANT CLASSIFICATION

Plants are found everywhere, in dry lands, in places with heavy rains, in hot and even in cold climates. They learn to adapt to their environment and the related changes. Plants are classified into **herbs**, **shrubs**, **trees** and **climbers**. However, plants can be placed in the following two major groups:

(i) Terrestrial plants, or plants that grow on land

(ii) Aquatic plants, or plants that grow in water

(i) Terrestrial Plants

These plants can be further divided based on the habitats, or the natural environment, in which they grow, such as:

- Deserts
- Hills
- Marshes
- Plains
- Forests
- Grasslands
- Coastal regions

Deserts

Palm Trees *Cactus Plants*

Plants found in the hot and dry climate of deserts adapt to their surroundings by obtaining water from the soil and preventing water loss from the surface of their leaves. It is a known fact that leaves have small pores on their surfaces. These pores are called stomata and the plants lose water through these pores. This process of losing water is called **transpiration**. However, desert plants, such as the cactus, lack such pores. They have pointed **spines** instead of leaves, reducing the loss of water from the surface. Such plants have an extensive root system that penetrates deep into the soil and absorbs water.

Hills

The hilly regions are generally cold. These areas are usually covered with snow. Surviving in such extreme climate is difficult for any plant. The plants of this region are however capable to withstand it. Trees, such as pines, have a conical shape, which helps the snow to slip off its surface. Its pointed leaves protect it from the harsh

Pine Tree

Cedar Tree

Spruce Trees

Deodar Tree

Fir Tree

winters. These plants have **cones** in place of flowers and are hence, often referred to as **conifers**. They are mostly **evergreen** and remain green throughout the year. Some other trees found in such areas are cedar, fir, deodar and spruce.

Marshes

Pickleweed

Marshes are formed of soil in the form of clay. Water gets trapped in the soil particles, making it muddy. The plants growing in these places can survive only if the roots can get fresh air and not get choked with water. Rabbit's foot grass and pickleweed are some of the examples of plants growing in marshes.

Plains

Maple Tree

Plains have a moderate climate. It's neither too cold nor too hot in the plains. They also receive sufficient rainfall. The plants growing in these regions are **deciduous** or

evergreen. The trees, such as maple, oak, birch, and beech, in the deciduous forests shed their leaves during winter and gain new leaves in spring.

Birch Tree *Oak Tree*

Beech Tree

Forests

Forests are densely populated with different varieties of trees, such as the *deciduous*, the *coniferous* and the *evergreen trees*.

Deciduous Trees *Evergreen Trees* *Coniferous Trees*

Grasslands

Tall Grass

Grasslands are so called as they are covered by grass. The length of the grasses may vary from very small grasses to really tall ones as in the **North American Prairies**, **African Savannas**, and the **South American Pampas** grasslands. The roots of these grasses are the potential source of food for many animals. These are the regions that receive more rainfall than the deserts, making them not too dry, and less rainfall than the rainforests, making them not wet enough for dense vegetation. Hence, the grasslands are generally covered by grass as well as non-woody plants. However, woody plants, trees, shrubs do grow in some grasslands.

Woody Plants

Coastal Regions

The coastal regions receive high rainfall and the water here is rich in salt content. Plants that mostly grow in these regions are coconut, rubber and pepper.

Rubber Plants

Coconut Tree

Pepper Plants

(ii) Aquatic Plants

There are three main types of aquatic plants:

- Floating aquatic plants
- Fixed aquatic plants
- Underwater aquatic plants

Water Hyacinth

Floating Aquatic Plants

Duckweed Plants

The plants which float on the surface of the water have to be light in weight in order to float. This is made possible by their spongy bodies full of air.

Fixed Aquatic Plants

Lotus

Some aquatic plants have their roots fixed to the ground under water. Since the roots are attached to the soil under water, they have to be flexible enough not to get damaged by the water currents. They have hollow stems and broad, flat leaves which help them to prepare their food using air and sunlight. Example, lotus.

Underwater Plants

Some plants are completely immersed in the water. These plants need to breathe under water. Unlike other plants, these plants have no stomata. They have tiny air sacs in their stems that help them to breathe.

Hydrilla

Other Plants

Most plants prepare their own food. However, there are many plants that depend on other green plants and trees for their food. Such plants are insectivorous, carnivorous, or parasites. Pitcher plants and Venus flytraps are insectivorous, whereas, Bladderworts are carnivorous underwater plants that trap animals for food. On the other hand, Mistletoes are the best examples of parasitic plants. They grow on other trees and suck the minerals and water from their host trees in order to survive.

Pitcher Plants

Mistletoes Growing on their Host Tree

Bladderworts

Venus Flytraps

Quick Facts

- Herbs are plants that have green and very soft stems as compared to other plants.They are terrestrial. Coriander are herbs.
- Rose and Bougainvillea are Shrubs. They have a thin, woody stem which is harder than that of the herbs, but not as hard as the tree trunks.
- Plants that have very hard, thick and woody stems, also called as trunks are called trees, such as Mango, Banyan, Apple, Guava.
- Money plant and Bottle Gourd are called climbers as they grow on big trees or on the walls of buildings and houses.
- Watermelon and cucumber are called creepers as they creep or crawl on the ground and do not grow straight like other plants.

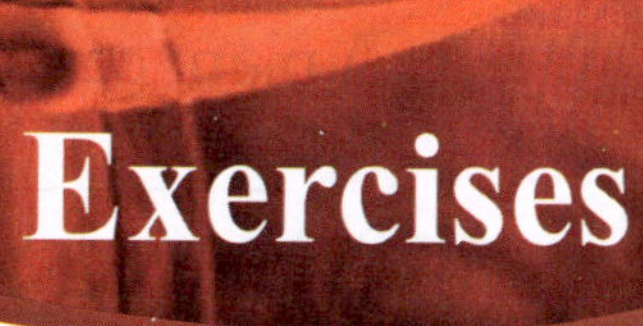

Exercises

I. Answer the following questions.

1. What is the difference between living and non-living things?
2. How do the living organisms breathe?
3. How do the living things move?
4. Why do the living organisms need food?
5. How do the plants prepare their food?
6. Why do the living things reproduce?
7. What are two major body systems in animals?
8. What are the main functions of the digestive and nervous systems in animals?
9. Explain the different parts of a plant with the help of a labelled diagram.
10. What is germination? Explain the process of germination in monocots and dicots with the help of diagrams.

II. Fill in the blanks with suitable words.

1. The animal kingdom is broadly classified into __________ and __________.
2. The muscular system helps in the __________ of the body using muscles.
3. Plants can be placed under two major groups: __________ and __________.

4. The process of losing water in plants is called ____________.
5. A plant can be divided into two major parts. The _____ and the ________.
6. Seeds are mainly of two types: ______________ and ______________.
7. A ________ is a place where an animal lives.
8. Depending upon their food habits, animals are divided into three groups: _______________ , ___________ and _______________.
9. The process of formation of seeds in plants is called ___________.
10. Pine, Cedar, Fir, Deodar and Spruce are also referred to as ________.

III. Match the two columns correctly.

	A	B
1.	The seasonal or annual journey of animals in search of better living conditions is called	floating aquatic plants.
2.	Water Hyacinth and Duckweed are examples of	Crustaceans, Arachnids and Insects.
3.	Lotus and Water Lily are examples of	Migration.
4.	Giraffes have no	fixed aquatic plants.
5.	Animals that live both on land and water are called	vocal chords.
6.	Antarctica is the only continent that does not have	Amphibians.

7. Tulsi, Mint and Coriander are	Reptiles and Snakes.
8. Arthropods can be divided into three groups:	called Herbs.
9. The largest flower in the world	in asexual reproduction.
10. An animal does not require a partner	is Rafflesia.

IV. Multiple Choice Questions (MCQs)

1. The respiratory system removes___________ which is harmful to the body.

   a. Carbon Dioxide b. Oxygen c. Nitrogen d. Ozone

2. Pollination starts from this part of the plant.

   a. Leaves b. Flower c. Root d. Stem

3. The young shoot of a plant is called a __________.

   a. Plumule b. Radicle c. Hypocotyl d. Epicotyl

4. There are some plants like __________ which do not have chlorophyll.

   a. Rose b. Hydrilla c. Rubber d. Mushrooms

5. The classification of animals is known as __________.

   a. Zoology b. Biology c. Taxonomy d. Ornithology

6. Man is an example of __________.

   a. Birds b. Reptiles c. Amphibians d. Mammals

7. Pitcher plants and Venus flytraps are examples of _______.

   a. Terrestrial plants b. Underwater plants

   c. Insectivorous plants d. None of these

8. Chameleons and Octopuses have the ability to change colour to merge with their surroundings. This is called as __________.

   a. Hunting b. Feeding c. Camouflage d. Migration

9. Frogs can see what is behind them without turning their __________.

   a. Heads b. Hands c. Backs d. Eyes

10. Fossils over millions of years old have proven that the ________were one of the first organisms on the earth.

V. State whether the following statements are True or False.

1. Birds, chickens and turtles lay eggs in which the young ones continue to develop. ☐
2. Fishes breathe with the help of their lungs. ☐
3. Reptiles are egg-laying animals. ☐
4. Predators hunt and kill other animals for food, while scavengers feed on the carcass or body of already dead animals. ☐
5. The internal skeleton is called Exoskeleton and the external skeleton is known as Endoskeleton. ☐
6. Insects, such as fly, mosquito, beetle, butterfly, moth, dragonfly, and bee form the largest group of Arthropods. ☐
7. The tall grasslands of Africa are called Prairies. ☐
8. Lotus and Water Lily are examples of fixed aquatic plants. ☐
9. No two zebras have exactly the same stripes. ☐
10. Fishes are the first backboned animals to appear on earth. ☐

Glossary

Adaptation: The act of adjusting to the changes happening in one's surrounding

Aerial: Existing or operating in the air as opposed to land or water

Altitude: Height above a reference point

Amphibians: Animals that live on land as well as in water

Annelids: Animals with segmented bodies, or bodies with rings, with no jointed legs

Anther: The male part of a flower consisting of pollen grains

Arthropod: Invertebrate animals with segmented bodies and no jointed legs

Aquatic: Animals or plants that live in water as opposed to land or air

Arachnids: Animals with segmented bodies divided into two regions and four pairs of legs but no antennae

Arboreal: Animals that live on trees in the open air

Arteries: Tubes that carry the pure blood away from the heart in a living organism's body

Asexual reproduction: The production of young ones without a partner

Camouflage: A form of defence mechanism, where an organism changes its body colour to blend into its surroundings, making it invisible to its attackers

Capillaries: The hair-like structures in the body that connect the small arteries and veins and form a network for the exchange of various substances in the body

Cardiovascular system: A body system formed by the organs and tissues that help to circulate blood in the body

Carnivores: Animals and plants that feed on animals

Cell: The smallest component of which an animal or plant body is made of

Cell membrane: The outer covering of a cell

Chlorophyll: The substance present in plants, giving them the green colour

Circulatory system: The body system responsible for blood circulation into all parts of the body

Climbers: Plants that have to take the support of trees or buildings to grow on account of their weak stems

Cold-blooded animals: Animals whose body temperature changes according to the temperature of their surroundings

Compound eyes: Eyes with more than one lens as opposed to that of human beings

Coniferous trees: Trees that produce cones instead of flowers

Cotyledon: The leaf of the embryo in a seed

Cross-pollination: Transfer of pollen grains from the male parts of a flower to the female parts of another flower

Crustaceans: A type of arthropods, called so because of their hard outer coverings

Deciduous trees: Trees that shed leaves in a season and gain new ones in another

Defence mechanisms: Tactics used by living beings to protect themselves from their attackers

Dicotyledons: Seeds with two cotyledons

Digestive system: The body system that helps in the conversion of food into energy

Echinoderms: Marine invertebrates that have outer skin covered with spines

Echolocation: A sensory system in some animals that helps them find their ways by listening to the sounds reflecting off from objects

Ecology: The scientific study of the relation between animals and their surroundings

Endocrine system: A body system that helps to control the activities of the body

Endoskeleton: The internal frame of the body of an animal

Endosperm: The covering of the embryo in the seed which provides food to the seed

Energy: The capacity of the body to perform

Epicotyl: The stem that grows between dicotyldons and first true leaves

Evergreen trees: Trees that do not shed leaves and remain green throughout the year

Excretory system: The body system that removes the waste material from the body

Exoskeleton: The hard outer covering that helps an animal to protect its soft internal organs

Extinction: The condition where a species stops existing or living

Fertilisation: The union of male and female organs to produce young ones

Fibrous root: A clump of thin hair-like roots

Filament: The thin stem-like structure in a flower that holds the anther

Food chain: The cycle formed by animals that feed upon the other

Fruit: The seed containing product of a plant

Fungi: Organisms that absorb food from other plants or the soil in which it grows and lacks chlorophyll

Germination: The process in which a seed grows into a plant

Gills: The respiratory organs in aquatic animals that help them to breathe in water

Habitat: An environment, where an animal lives for most part of the year

Herbivores: Animals that feed on plants, trees, grasses

Hormones: Substances produced by internal organs that affect the functions of the body

Hypocotyl: Part of the plant embryo in a seed below the cotyledons

Inhabitant: The permanent resident of a place

Insectivores: Animals or plants that feed on insects

Invertebrates: Animals with no backbones

Larva: The young one of an insect that does not have wings and goes through a complete transformation as it grows

Leaf: The part of a plant that produces food and is usually green in colour

Mammal: Animals that feed their young ones using their mammary glands

Mammary gland: The milk-producing part of a female mammal

Migration: The temporary but regular journey taken by an animal in search of food or better living conditions

Molluscs: Invertebrates that have soft, unsegmented bodies and often have shells or hard outer coverings

Monocotyledon: Any flowering plant with one cotyledon

Multi-cellular animals: Animals having many cells

Muscular system: The body system that controls the movement of the body

Nervous system: The body system that manages the information sent to the body by internal and external factors

Omnivores: Animals that feed on both animals and plants

Ovary: The female part of a plant

Ovule: A product of the ovary that develops into a seed after fertilisation

Parasites: Animals or plants that feed on a living, host animal or plant for their own survival

Petal: The part of a flower that attracts insects and birds and helps in pollination

Photosynthesis: The process of producing food in plants using sunlight, carbon dioxide, and water.

Pistil: The organ of a flower that contains the ovule

Plumule: The young stem that grows from a seed during germination

Pollen grain: The dust-like material produced by the anther of a flower

Pollination: The transfer of pollen from the male parts of the flower to the female parts through wind, animals, birds, insects

Predators: Animals that attack other animals for food

Protozoa: Single-celled organisms that can only be seen under a microscope

Radicle: Young root that develops during the germination of the seed

Rainforest: A dense evergreen forest that receives a lot of rain

Reproductive system: The body system that helps in the production of the young ones

Respiratory system: The body system the helps the organism to breathe

Root: The underground part of a plant that holds the plant firmly to the soil and absorbs water and nutrients from the soil and sends it to the stem

Scavengers: Animals that feed on the dead bodies of other animals or plants

Self-pollination: The transfer of pollen from the male to the female parts of the same flower

Sense organs: Organs that let and help an organism eat, breathe, feel, see, hear, or touch

Sepal: The green leaf-like structure below that connects the flower to the stem

Sexual reproduction: The process of producing a young one with the help of a partner

Shoot: The part of a plant above the ground

Single-celled animals: Animals with one cell each

Skeletal system: The body system that supports the body giving it a strong internal or external frame

Spinal chord: The main backbone of an animal

Stamen: The pollen-producing organ of the flower that contains the anther and the filament

Stem: The part of a plant or a tree that distributes water gained from the roots to different parts of the plant and helps in the production of branches, leaves, flowers and fruits

Stigma: The reproductive part of a flower to which the pollen sticks

Stomata: The small pore-like structures under the leaves that help the plants to breathe

Streamlined: Shaped like a boat, broad in the middle and pointed at both ends

Tap root: Root system with one main root, broad at one end and tapered at the other, with many thin roots on its sides

Terrestrial: Animals or plants that live on land

Testa: The outer covering of a seed

Transpiration: The process of losing water in plants

Veins: The thin tube-like structures that carry impure blood from different parts of a body to the heart, or thin hair- like structures in a leaf that distribute water to different parts of a leaf

Vertebrates: Animals with a backbone

Warm-blooded animals: Animals that can maintain a steady body temperature and are not affected by the outside temperature

Wetlands: Lands with wet and spongy soil

THE HUMAN BODY

The human body is the entire structure of a human organism, and consists of a head, neck, torso, two arms and two legs. By the time, the human being (man or woman) reaches adulthood, the body consists of close to *100 trillion cells*, the basic unit of life. These cells are organised biologically to eventually form the whole body.

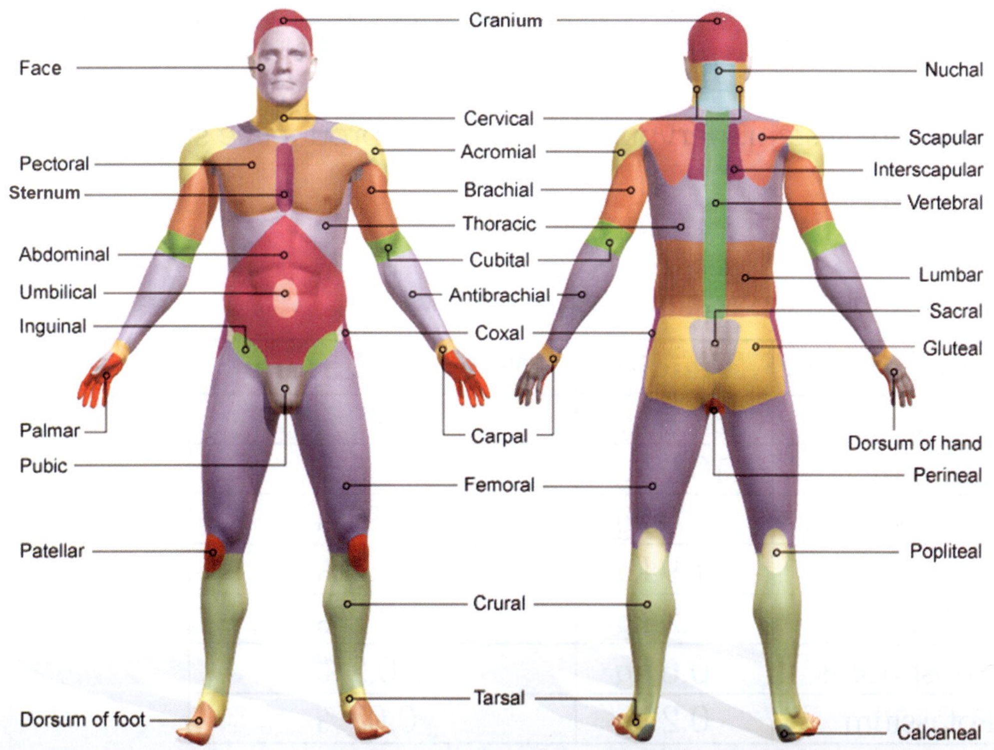

Parts of the Body

Size, Type and Proportion

The average height of an adult male human is about 1.7–1.8 m (5'7" to 5'11") tall and the adult female about 1.6–1.7 m (5'2" to 5'7") tall. This size is firstly determined by genes and secondly, by diet. Body type and body composition are influenced by post-natal factors such as diet and exercise.

Organ Systems

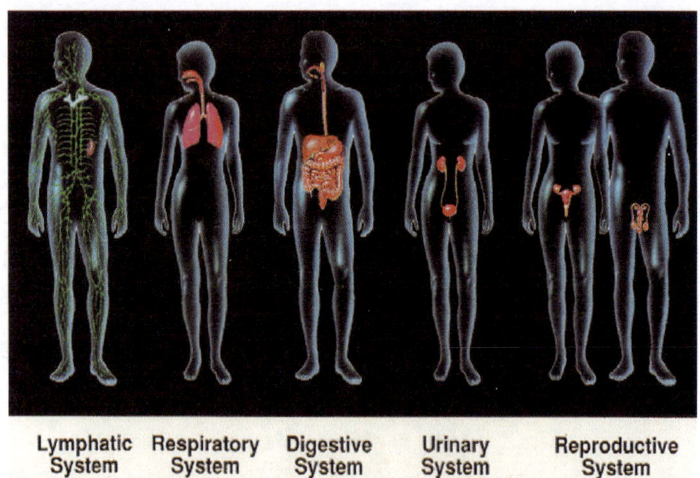

The organ systems of the body include the musculoskeletal system, cardiovascular system, digestive system, endocrine system, integumentary system, urinary system, lymphatic system, immune system, respiratory system, nervous system and reproductive system.

Constituents of Human Body

In a normal man weighing 60 kg

Constituents	Weight	Percent of atoms
Oxygen	38.8 kg	25.5%
Carbon	10.9 kg	9.5%
Hydrogen	6.0 kg	63%
Nitrogen	1.9 kg	1.4%
Calcium	1.2 kg	0.2%
Phosphorus	0.6 kg	0.2%
Potassium	0.2 kg	0.07%

Part - I

THE INTERNAL ORGANS

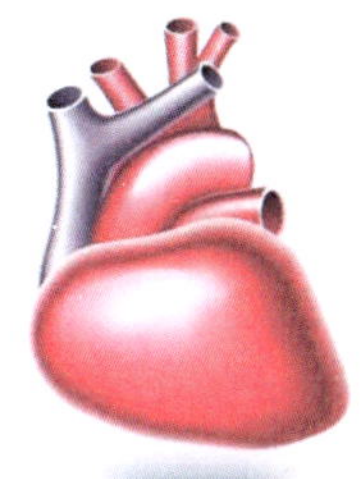

Heart

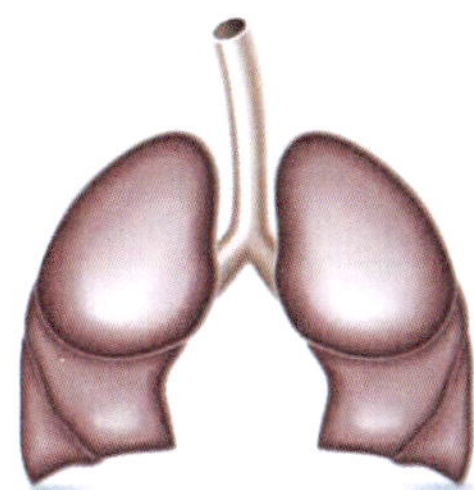

Lungs

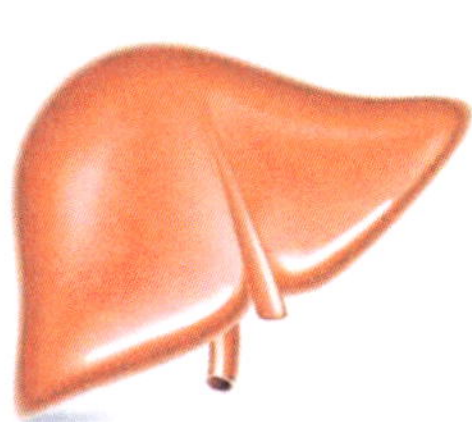

Liver

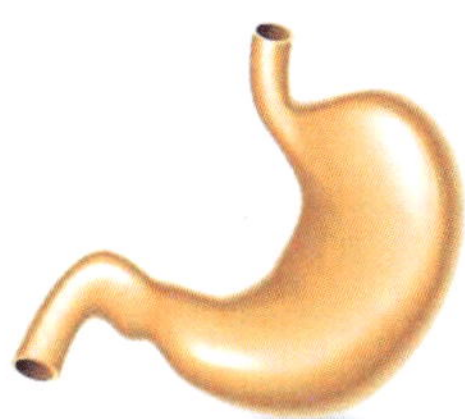

Stomach

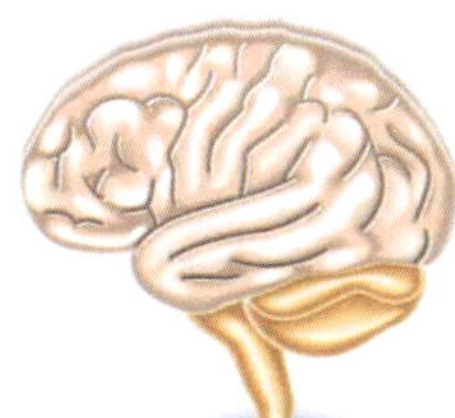

Brain

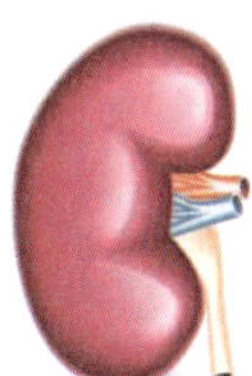

Kidneys

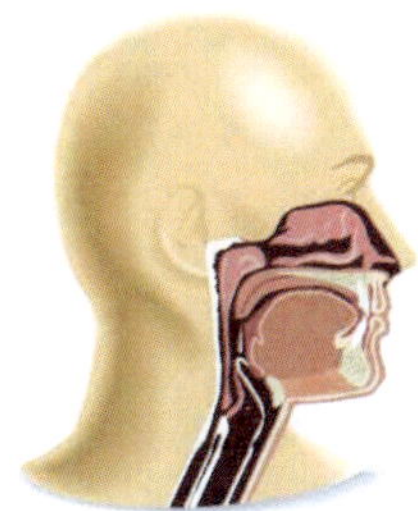

Trachea and Oesophagus

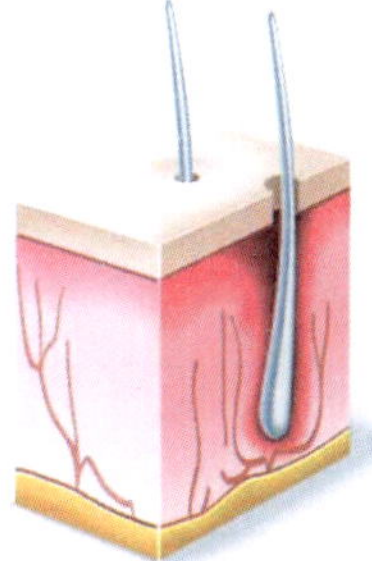

Skin

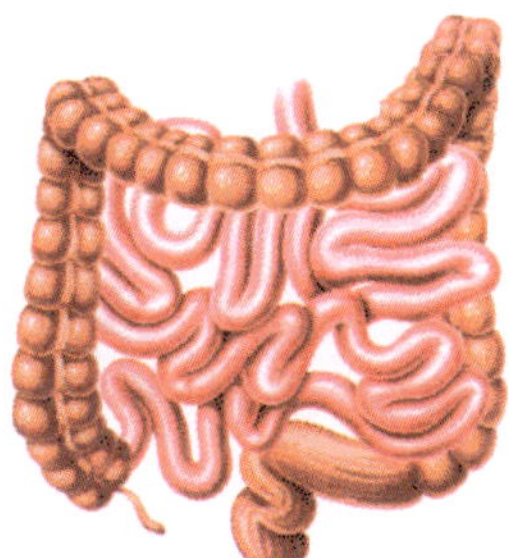

Small Intestine

Chapter - 1

THE CELLS

The human body is formed by millions of tiny units called *cells*. Each of these tiny units has a specific shape, size and function to perform. There are more than 200 types of cells known till today. These cells function together and perform all the actions of the human body. The millions of cells in the body practise division of labour and hence, various groups of cells perform the different functions of the human body. Cells that perform a particular function together are called tissues.

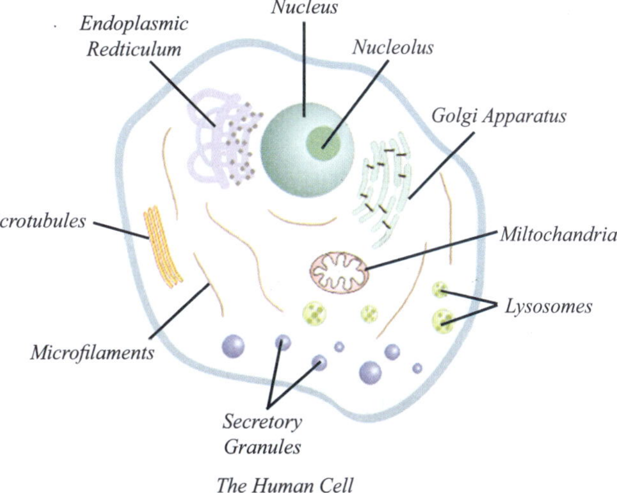

The Human Cell

A thin membrane, called as the cell membrane, surrounds each individual cell. It performs the job of regulating things like nutrients and other substances in and out of the cell. Cells multiply by dividing continually into two identical offsprings. It is through this division process that the body is able to grow and replace the damaged or worn out cells.

The broad categories of the kinds of cells in the human body are:

1. Nerve Cells

These are one of the most important kinds of cells in the body. These are called **Neurons**, and are found in the *brain*, *spinal cord* and the *nerves*. They are responsible for carrying high-speed electrical signals, called nerve impulses. It is due to these impulses that our body processes, coordinates and we are able to think, feel and move. There are two types of nerves functioning in the human body. The *Sensory Nerves* which contain the Sensory Nerve Cells bringing signals and information to the brain and the **Motor Nerves** containing the Motor Nerve Cells carrying orders and messages from the brain to the various organs and parts of the body.

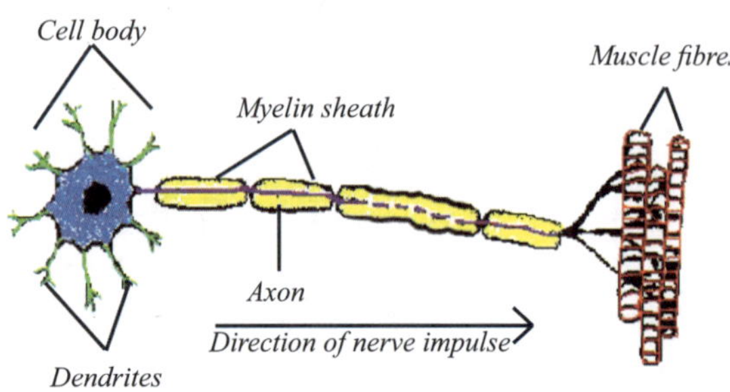

Nerve Cell or Neuron

2. White Blood Cells (WBCs)

These cells are called the soldiers of the human body. Circulating in the *blood* and a clear fluid called *lymph*, these cells are responsible for fighting the diseases that attack the human body. These cells consist of *macrophages* and *neutrophils*, which perform the job of eating bacteria and other germs. Also, these cells contain **lymphocytes**, which release germ-disabling antibodies.

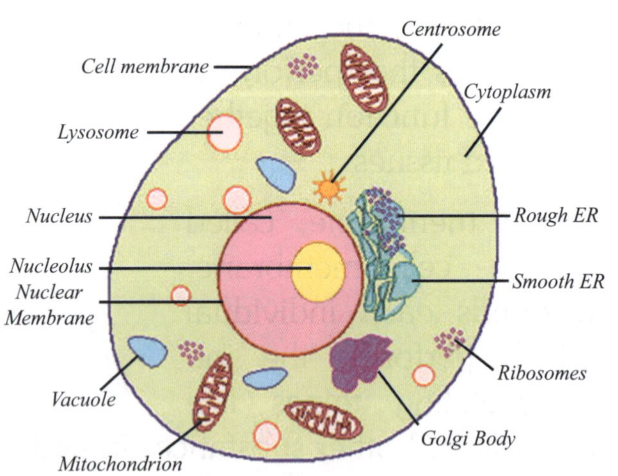

White Blood Cells (WBCs)

3. Red Blood Cells (RBCs)

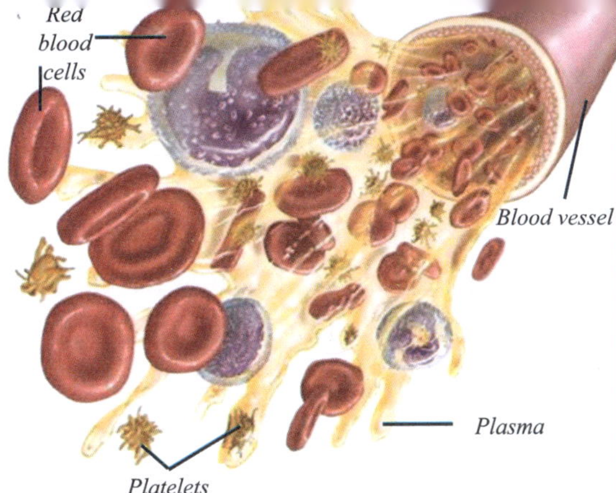

Red Blood Cells (RBCs)

The Red blood cells, or Erythrocytes, are the most common type of blood cells, and the vertebrate organism's principal means of delivering oxygen (O_2) to the body tissues through the blood flow or the circulatory system. They take up oxygen in the lungs or gills and release it while squeezing through the body's capillaries. These cells' cytoplasm is rich in **haemoglobin**, an iron-containing biomolecule that can bind oxygen and is responsible for the blood's red colour.

In humans, mature red blood cells are oval and flexible biconcave disks. They lack a cell nucleus and most organelles to accommodate maximum space for haemoglobin. About 2.4 million new **erythrocytes** are produced per second. The cells develop in the bone marrow and circulate for about 100–120 days in the body before their components are recycled by macrophages. Each circulation takes about 20 seconds. Approximately, a quarter of the cells in the human body are **Red Blood Cells** or **RBCs**.

4. Epithelial Cells

These cells cover the human body as they form the outer layer of the skin. They also line the hollow organs, such as the stomach, lungs and the bladder. These are tightly packed together and are responsible for stopping harmful chemicals and germs from reaching the body tissues.

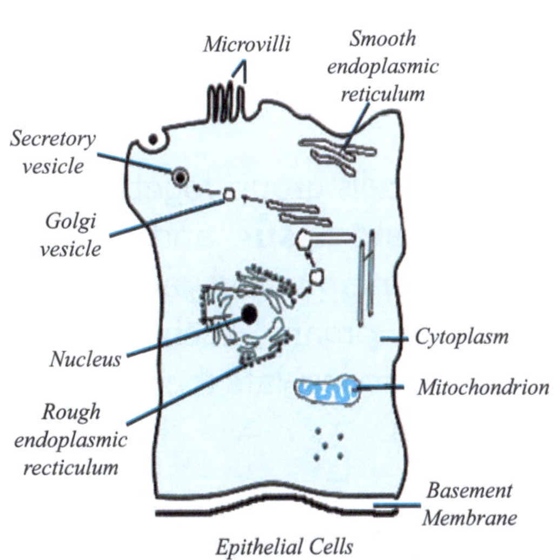

Epithelial Cells

5. Bone Cells or Osteocytes

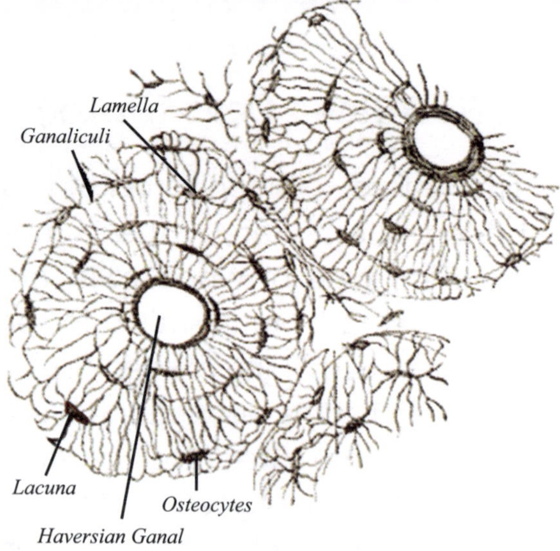

Bone Cells or Osteocytes

These are the bone cells that help keep the bones in a good condition. They primarily lay down as bones, but later get stranded in the body spaces. They stay connected through thread like veins and arteries, and blood supplies from the surrounding blood vessels.

6. Liver Cells or Hepatocytes

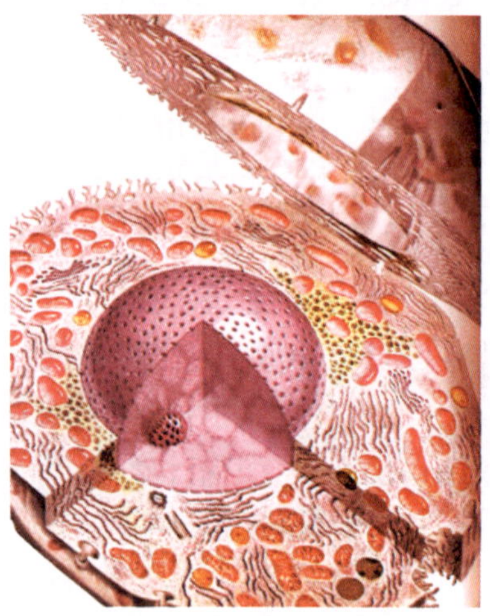
Liver cells or Hepatocytes

These cells are responsible for enabling the liver to perform functions, such as controlled blood composition and maintain stability in the body. Also called as **Hepatocytes**, they process and stored food and remove the poisonous waste from the liver.

7. Fat Cells

These cells group together to form the **Adipose tissue** and store fat. They store energy and also cushion the various organs, such as the kidneys. They also insulate the body from under the skin.

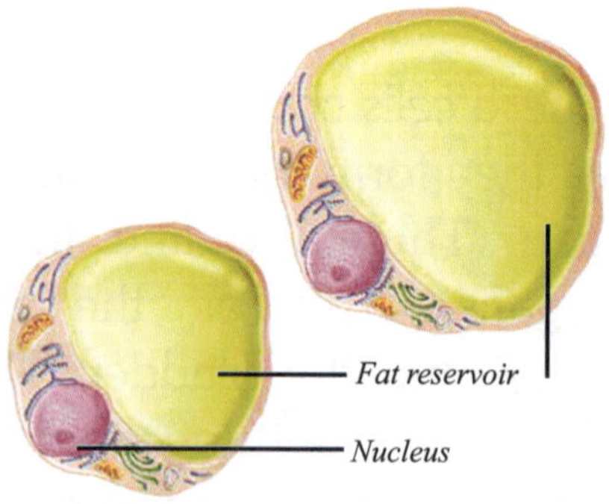

Fat Cells

Quick Facts

- One can grow heart cells in a petri dish.
- The human body is made up of 100 trillion cells. Each cell has at least one nucleus, which houses the chromosomes.
- There is 1.8 m of DNA in each of our cells packed into a structure only 0.0001 cm across (it would easily fit on the head of a pin).
- If all the DNA in the 100 trillion cells of the human body was put end to end, it would reach to the sun and back over 600 times [100 trillion × 6 ft (1.8 m) divided by 92 million miles (148 800 000 km) = 1200].
- Most human cells contain 46 chromosomes: pairs of chromosomes 1-22, and a pair of sex chromosomes (females have two Xs; males have an X and a Y). The sperm and eggs contain one of each chromosome.

Chapter - 2

BLOOD

The red liquid flowing all around our body is called blood. It is probably the most important part of the human body as it is the blood that performs the most vital functions of the body. Circulating in **arteries** and **veins**, the blood carries *food, oxygen* and other *essential substances* around the body. It also carries cells and removes their wastes. Moreover, it is responsible for providing heat to the body and defends it against diseases and infections. In an average human body, around **5 litres** of blood circulates at any given time.

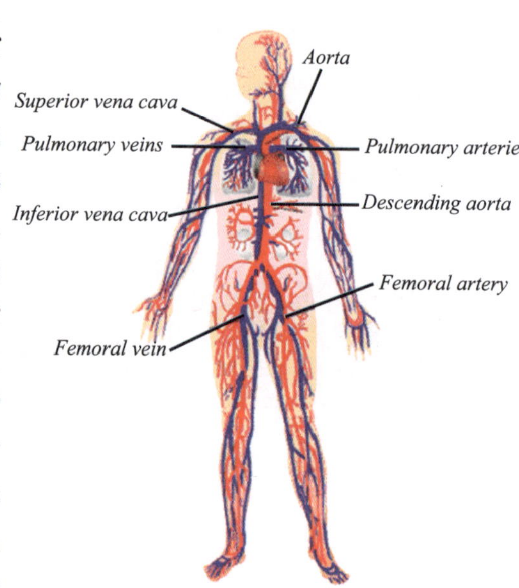

Circulatory System of the Human Body

The human blood is made of a yellow liquid called the **plasma**. The plasma is formed of 90% water and the rest 10% consists of various dissolved substances like food, salts, hormones, etc. Further, the blood consists of 55% plasma and the rest is constituted of blood cells.

Various blood cells perform different functions. The **Red Blood Cells (RBCs)** carry oxygen from the lungs to the rest of the body. Every second, two million Red Cells are produced in the human body. The **White Blood Cells (WBCs)**, called *neutrophils* and *macrophages* eat germs and protect us against diseases. They release antibodies that fight germs in our body.

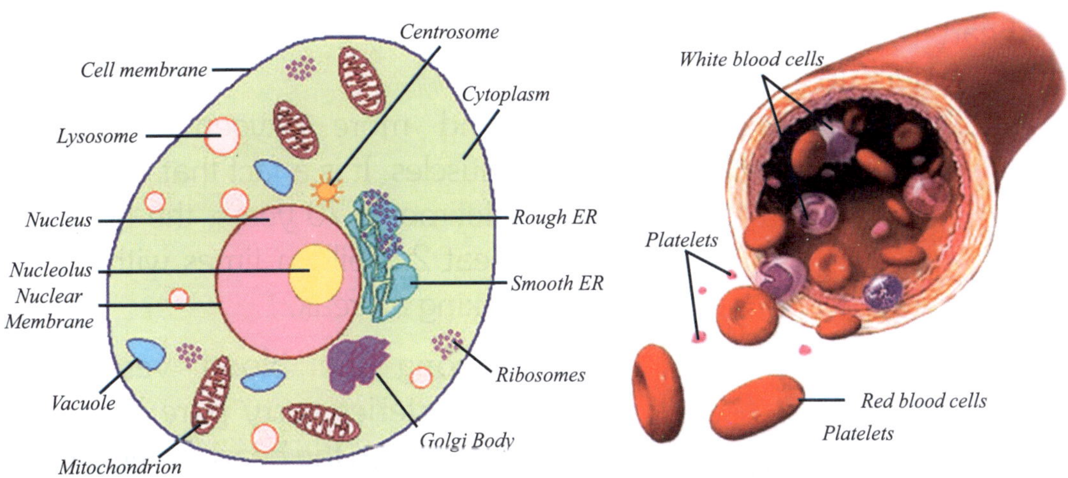

White Blood Cells (WBCs)

Another element of the blood, called the **platelets** perform the job of clotting the damaged blood vessels. It is interesting to know that each drop of blood consists of about 250 million Red Blood Cells (RBCs), around 375,000 White Blood Cells (WBCs) and 1 million platelets.

The **heart** pumps the blood. The human heart is made up of mainly *cardiac muscles* which do not tire. The **veins** bring deoxygenated blood to the heart which then oxygenates it and pumps out to the body through the **arteries**. On an average, the human heart beats **72 times in a minute**.

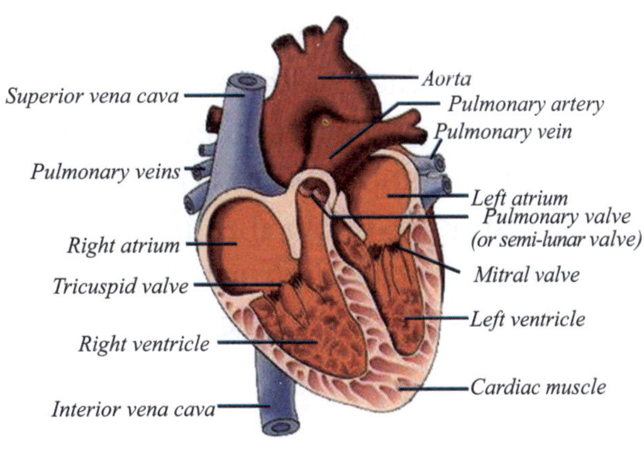

Human Heart Pumping Blood

However, this rating may increase to double or even triple due to excessive physical activity and then, the heart pumps blood faster to

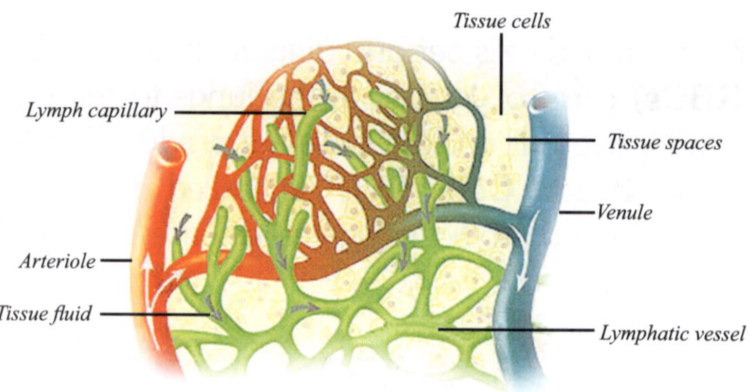

Capillaries

send more oxygen to our muscles. It is a fact that over a lifetime of 70 years, the heart beat 2.5 billion times without taking a break.

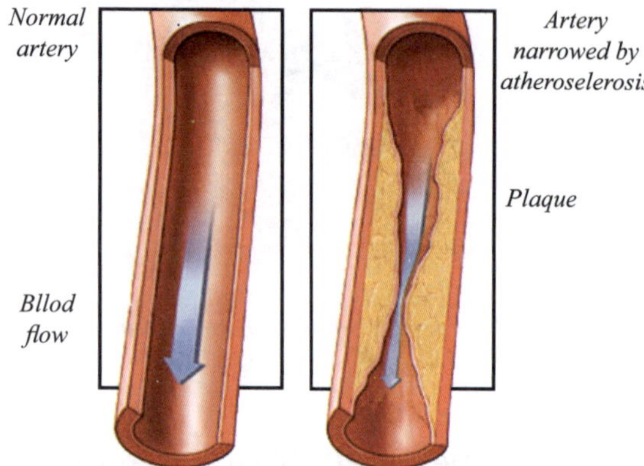

Artery

Among the blood vessels, the arteries carry pure blood away from the heart, while the veins bring the impure blood from the different organs back to it. Microscopic **capillaries** link the arteries and veins to provide blood to the cells. The arteries carry bright-red coloured blood as it is oxygenated, whereas the veins carry the deoxygenated blood, which is dull-purple in colour. It is interesting to know that if stretched out, one adult's blood vessels would encircle the Earth twice and the capillaries would make up about 98 percent of the total length.

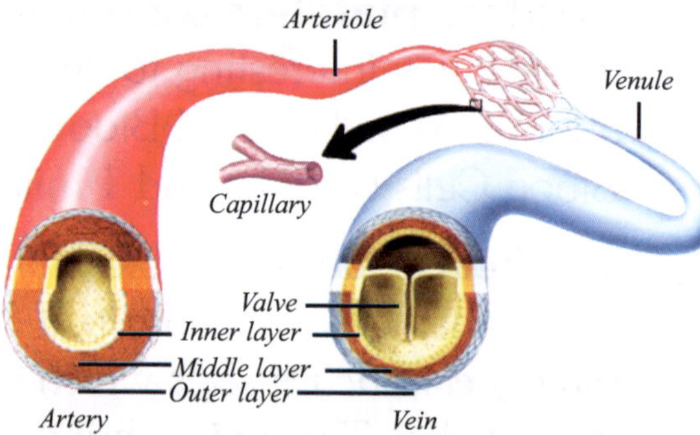

Blood Vessel

Quick Facts

- Blood makes up around 10 percent of our body weight. Our weight divided by 12 tells us how many pints of blood our body has.
- Blood cells float in a yellow liquid called blood plasma. This is made up of 90% water and also contains various nutrients, proteins, glucose and hormones.
- Blood is about twice as thick as water, due to all the cells and other bits that float in it.
- Blood makes up about 10 percent of your body weight. Weigh yourself and divide your weight by 12 — that answer is about how many pints of blood your body has. Adults usually have roughly 10 to 15 pints. A newborn baby has about one-half pint or one cup of blood.
- It takes roughly 20 to 60 seconds for the blood to travel away from the heart and back again.

Chapter - 3

THE BRAIN

The brain is one of the most vital organs of the human body. Resting inside the skull, it enables us to *think*, *sense*, *learn*, *move* and *remember*. It also regulates other important processes of the body, such as breathing.

The main part of the human brain, called the **cerebrum** is divided into two hemispheres. While the right hemisphere controls the left side of the body and deals with art, music and creativity, the left side, controls the right side of the body and is responsible for mathematics, language and problem solving. The outer layer of the cerebrum, known as the **cortex**, performs all its tasks. The cortex has different roles at distinct areas of the brain. So,

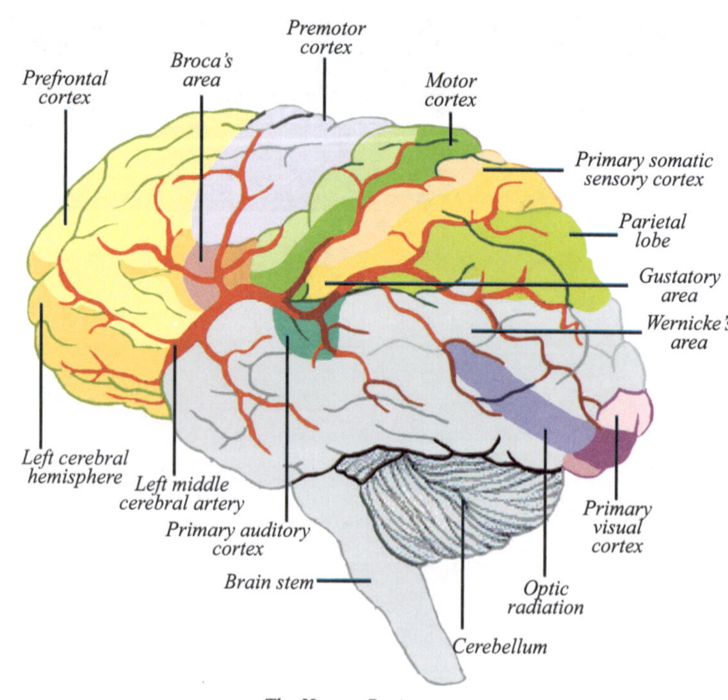

The Human Brain

the motor areas trigger movements, the association areas interpret functions, the sensory areas deal with senses and so on.

Some of the parts of the Brain and their functions are as follows:

1. **Prefrontal Cortex:** This is the most complex part of the cerebrum and is responsible for what we are. It allows us to reason, plan, create and learn about thoughts and ideas and gives us the sense of having a *conscience*. Hence, it is responsible for our personality and intellect.
2. **Broca's area:** This is usually placed in the left hemisphere, and is responsible for *planning* what we are about to say and accordingly sends out instructions to the muscles in the throat, tongue and lips to produce speech. It was named after *Dr. Paul Broca*, who discovered it.
3. **Premotor Cortex:** This part of the brain controls all the *movement skills*, for example, playing tennis or swimming, etc. At the time of physical movement, it instructs the specific muscles to contract, etc. either through the primary motor cortex or directly.
4. **Primary Motor Cortex:** Most of the movement of the human body is regulated by the primary motor cortex. It *receives information* from the *cerebellum* and other parts of the brain and instructs the muscles to move and in a particular sequence.
5. **Cerebellum:** This part of the human brain performs the task of enabling *smooth and coordinated movements*. After analysing the incoming information about the body's current position, it interacts with the primary motor cortex to time the muscle contractions precisely.
6. **Primary Visual Cortex:** As light hits the back of the retina in each eye, the light detectors send a signal to the primary visual cortex. It then *interprets* the basic shapes, sizes and colour and passes it on to the visual association cortex.

7. **Visual Association Cortex:** This is the place where *information* of the primary visual cortex is analysed and *compared* to previous experiences. It identifies what and where we are looking, enabling us to actually see things.

8. **Primary Sensory Cortex:** There are receptors in our skin which send signals regarding touch, vibration, etc. enabling us to *feel* them. Lips and fingertips have more receptors and hence, they are extra sensitive.

9. **Sensory Association Cortex:** The information about touch or any kind of sensation is passed to the sensory association cortex by the primary sensory cortex. It is then *analysed and interpreted* before being compared to past experiences.

10. **Primary Auditory Cortex:** Sounds detected by the ears are transferred to the primary auditory cortex, where the *loudness, pitch, etc. are identified*. Then the information is passed to the auditory association cortex.

11. **Auditory Association Cortex:** This is where *sounds* are actually *heard*. Using signals from the primary auditory cortex, it joins the pieces together to form complete sounds and *identifies* it as music, speech.

12. **Wernicke's Area:** It is usually found in the left hemisphere of the cerebrum, it gives meaning to the words that are heard or read. It is directly linked to the Broca's area, which enables speech.

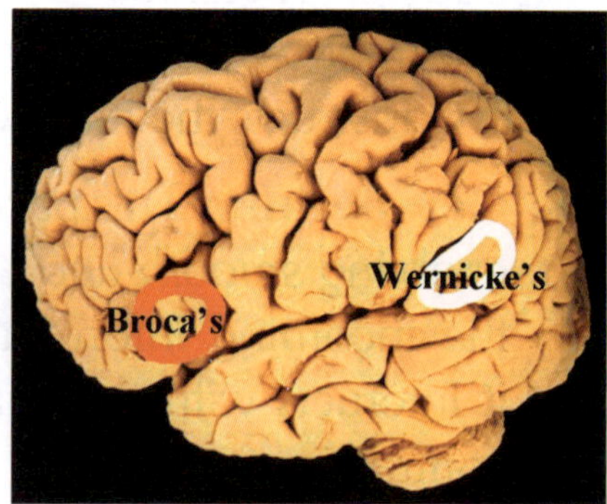

Wernicke's Area of the Cerebrum

Quick Facts

- The human brain is like a powerful computer that stores our memory and controls how we as humans think and react. It has evolved over time and features some incredibly intricate parts that scientists still struggle to understand.
- The brain can process information as slowly as 0.5 metres/sec or as fast as 120 metres/sec.
- The brain is the centre of the human nervous system, controls our thoughts, movements, memories and decisions.
- The brain contains billions of nerve cells that send and receive information around the body.
- The human brain is over three times as big as the brain of other mammals that are of similar body size.

THE SENSES

The human body constitutes of **five senses** which enable us to be a part of the world around us and observe and notice the changes that occur in it. Our eyes and ears detect *light waves* and *sound waves* respectively. These allow us to see and hear. The tongue and the nose perform the task of detecting dissolved chemicals so that we can *taste, smell* and hence, enjoy flavours. The skin allows us to *feel* the texture and *warmth* of the objects that surround us.

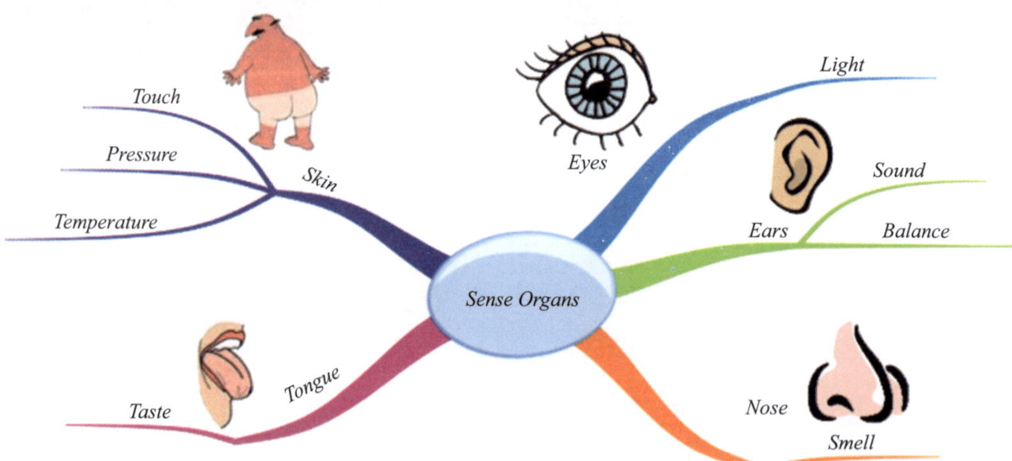

Vision

This is the most important sense as it provides the brain immense amount of knowledge about the body's surroundings. The light that

is reflected or produced by objects that surround us is focussed on a layer of light receptors that exist at the back of our *eyes*. These receptors send the light signals to the back of the brain, where the images are developed and interpreted. Signals are then sent back to the *eye*, enabling us to *see* objects around us.

Hearing

The receptors in the ears detect the waves of pressure, or *sound waves* that travel through the air. These waves are created by things around us, like a bell ringing or a mobile phone vibrating.

These waves pass into the inner part of the ear which is enclosed in a bone at the side of the skull. This is where the *receptors* convert the *waves into signals* that travel through the brain. The brain then interprets the *loudness*, *pitch*, etc. and completes the sound for us to hear.

Taste

Our tongue has got numerous projections on its surface, called the *papillae*. These are a home to the taste receptors, called the *taste buds*. When food molecules dissolve in *saliva*, the taste buds detect them. Taste can be distinguished as *sweet, bitter, sour, salty*, etc. Apart from tasting, these receptors also help us to detect any kind of poison that may be present in the food.

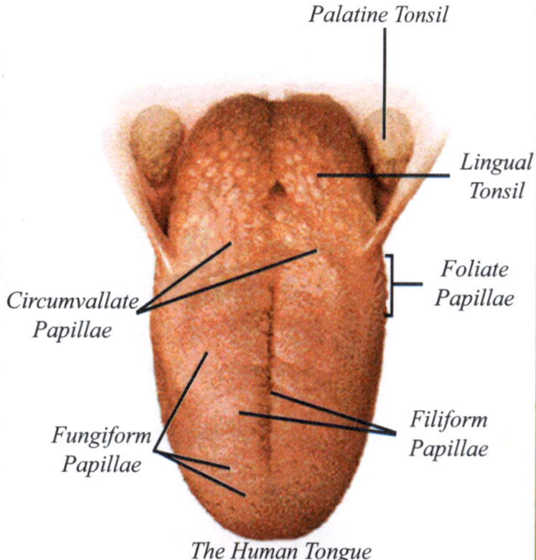

The Human Tongue

Touch

Human *skin* is like a sense organ. It has got innumerable receptors all over its surface, enabling us to feel our surroundings. Most of these are *touch receptors* that send signals to the brain and allow us to feel things. Other receptors pick up changes in *temperature*.

Smell

It is a fact that the human nose can detect up to *10,000 different smells*. When we breathe air, the odour molecules dissolved in mucus act as receptors and pick up the smell. Together, taste and smell enable us to enjoy flavours. This is the reason why food seems flavourless when we have a blocked nose.

Quick Facts

- **After eating, our hearing power decreases.**
- **About one-third of the human race has 20-20 vision. Glasses and contact wearers are hardly alone in a world where two thirds of the population have less than perfect vision. The amount of people with perfect vision decreases further as they age.**
- **If our saliva cannot dissolve something, we cannot taste it. In order for foods or anything else, to have a taste, chemicals from the substance must be dissolved by saliva. If you don't believe it, try drying off your tongue before tasting something.**
- **Your nose can remember about 50,000 different scents.**

PART - II

OUR BODY SYSTEMS

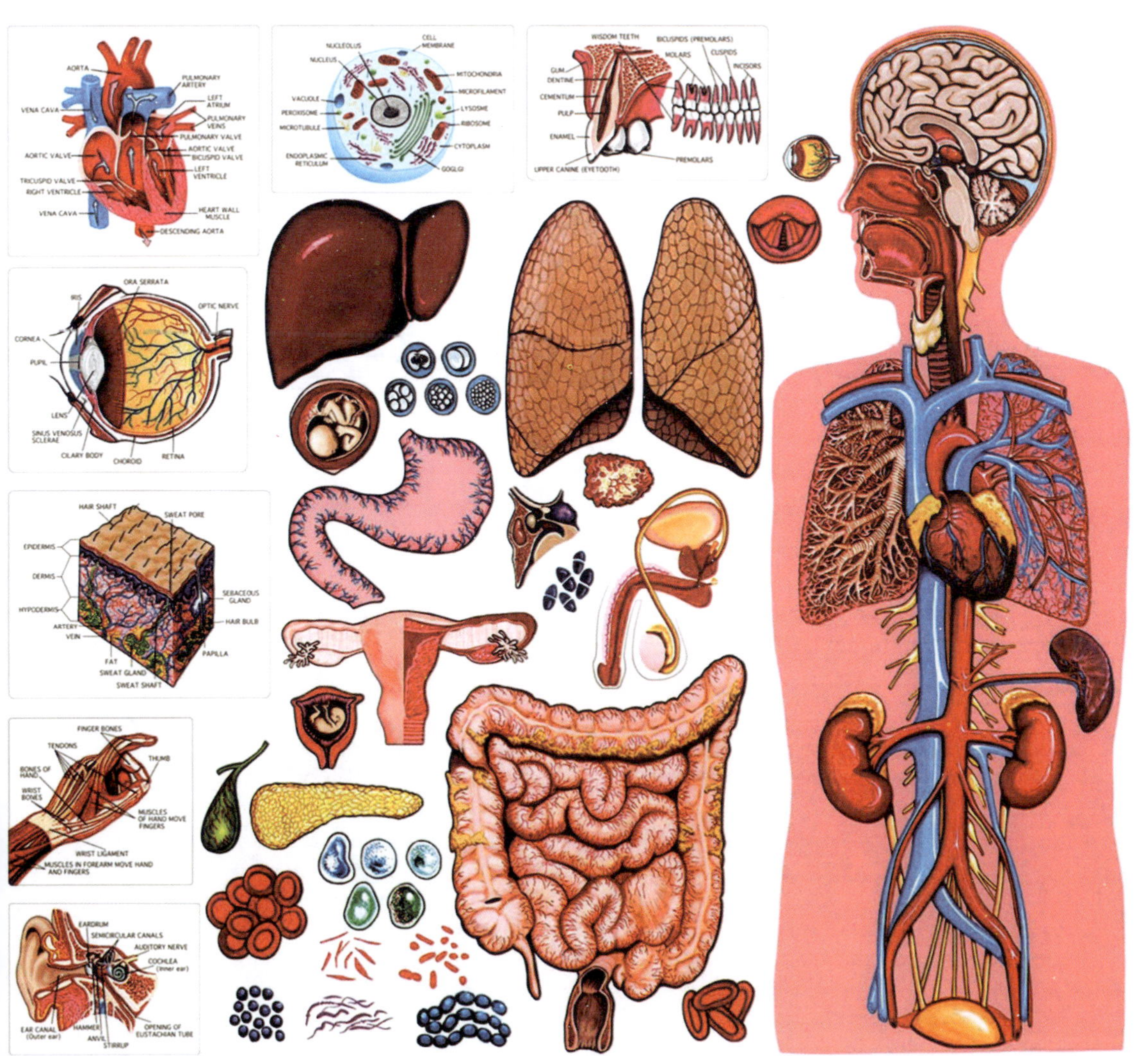

Chapter - 1

THE RESPIRATORY SYSTEM

The respiratory system of our body is responsible for one of major functions of the body. It is through this process that the trillion of cells in our body receive oxygen that they need to survive. In a broad sense, oxygenated air is breathed into the body by the respiratory system. Air with **oxygen** reaches the blood through lungs and is further carried to the blood cells, while the waste **carbon dioxide** is carried by the blood to the lungs and breathed out.

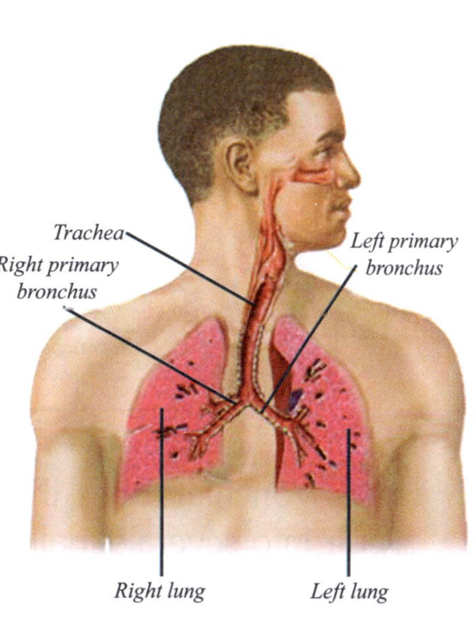

Respiratory System

The prime responsibility of the respiratory system is to *supply blood with oxygen*. The blood then delivers this oxygen to various parts of the body. The respiratory system does this through the process of **breathing**. When we breathe, we *inhale oxygen* and *exhale carbon dioxide* and it is through this exchange of gases that the respiratory system is able to get oxygen into the blood.

The process of respiration involves the use of the *mouth*, *nose*, *trachea*, *lungs*, and the *diaphragm*. Oxygen enters the human body through the mouth and the nose. It then passes through the larynx, the area where speech sounds are produced and the trachea which is basically a tube like structure that leads to the chest cavity. Here, the trachea splits into two small tubes. These are called the *bronchi*. Each bronchus further divides into various *bronchial tubes*. It is

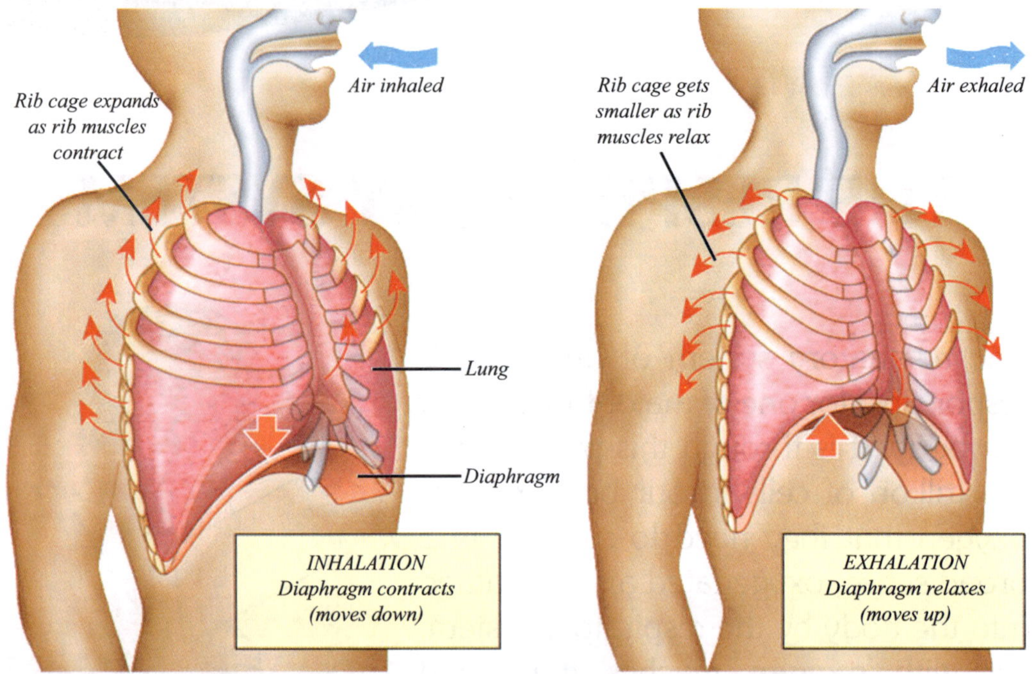

The Process of Inhaling Oxygen and Exhaling Carbon Dioxide in the Human Body

these bronchial tubes that lead directly into the lungs. They then divide into several smaller tubes which are connected to tiny sacs called the *alveoli*. It is an interesting fact that an average adult's lungs contain about 600 million of these spongy, air-filled sacs. The alveoli are surrounded by *capillaries*.

The oxygen we inhale passes into alveoli, where it diffuses into the arterial blood, through the capillaries. During this time, the waste-rich blood from the veins releases its carbon dioxide into the alveoli. This carbon dioxide then goes out of the body through the same path, when we exhale.

It is the job of the *diaphragm* to help pump out carbon dioxide from the lungs and pull oxygen into the body. The diaphragm is like a sheet of muscles, lying across the bottom of the chest cavity. The process of breathing occurs as the *contraction* and *expansion* of the diaphragm occurs. At the time of contraction, oxygen is pulled into the lungs. On the other hand, when the diaphragm relaxes, carbon dioxide is pumped out of the lungs.

Together all these parts perform to ensure that the blood is circulated throughout the body and hence, the *cells are supplied with adequate amount of oxygen* to make life possible on the Earth.

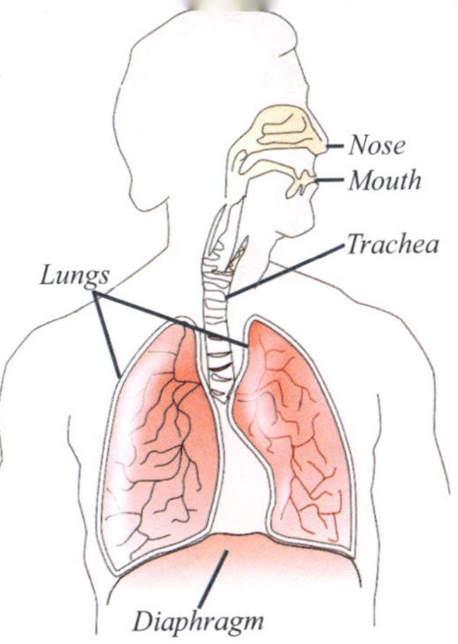

Human Diaphragm

Quick Facts

- We breathe around 6.5 litres of air each minute.
- There are 1500 miles of airways in the human respiratory system.
- The right lung is slightly larger than the left.
- Hairs in the nose help to clean the air we breathe as well as make it warm.
- The highest recorded "sneeze speed" is 165 km per hour.
- The surface area of the lungs is roughly of the same size as a tennis court.
- The capillaries in the lungs would extend to 1,600 km if placed end to end.
- We lose half a litre of water a day through breathing. This is the water vapour we see when we breathe onto glass.
- A person at rest usually breathes between 12 and 15 times a minute.
- The breathing rate is faster in children and women than in men.

Chapter - 2

THE EXCRETORY SYSTEM

The job of the excretory system is to remove waste products from the body. It removes both solid wastes and fluids. The parts of the excretory system are:

- **The kidneys**: *It filters and takes the waste out of the blood, and makes urine.*

The main organs of this system are:

- **The ureters**: *These are tubes that carry the urine to the bladder.*
- **The bladder**: *It is a bag like structure that collects the urine.*
- **The urethra**: *This is a tube that carries the urine out of the body.*

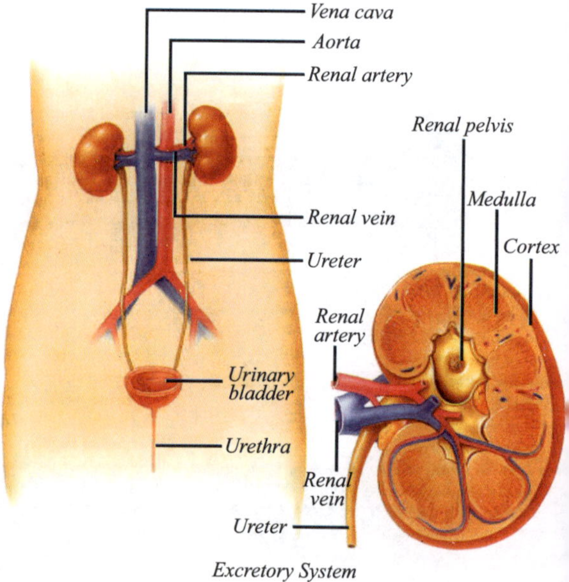

Excretory System

Functions of the Kidneys

One of the main jobs of the kidneys is to filter the waste out of the blood. These waste products may be a result of chemical reactions which occur from the breaking down of nutrients in our body. They may also be something which the body doesn't require because it already has enough of it. All these waste products have to be thrown out. That is the responsibility of excretory system.

How is blood cleaned up?

First, the blood is carried into the kidneys by the *renal artery* (anything in the body related to the kidneys is called 'renal'). The kidney filters this blood about 400 times in a day. More than a million tiny filters called *nephrons* remove waste products.

The waste that is collected combines with water (which is also filtered out of the kidneys) to make *urine*. As each kidney makes urine, the urine slides down a long tube called the *ureter* and collects in the *bladder*, a storage sac that holds the urine. When the bladder is about halfway full, your body tells you to go to the bathroom. When you pee, the urine goes from the bladder down another tube called the *urethra* and out of your body.

The kidneys also balance the volume of fluids and minerals in the body. This balance is called *homeostasis*. If you don't have enough fluids in your body, the brain communicates with the kidneys by sending out a hormone that tells the kidneys to hold on to some fluids. When you drink more, this hormone level goes down, and the kidneys will let go off more fluids.

The kidneys constantly react to the hormones that the brain sends them. The kidneys even make some of their own hormones. For example, the kidneys produce a hormone that tells the body to make the Red Blood Cells (RBCs).

Problems of the Kidneys

The kidneys are extremely vital organs. While there are many diseases of the excretory system, even more problems can be created by malfunctioning of kidneys. **Blood pressure** is closely tied to the amount of fluid in your body. If a kidney does not work and filter properly, blood pressure can increase to dangerous levels. Also, **urea** would accumulate in your tissues and would slowly poison the cells of your body.

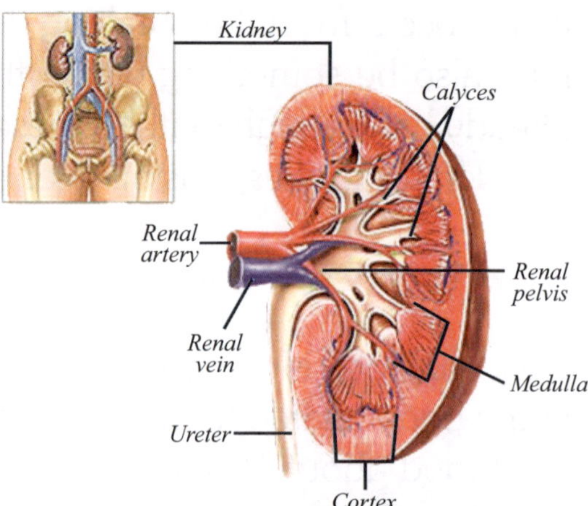

People with malfunctioning kidneys often have to go through a process called **dialysis**, where they are hooked up to a machine that filters their blood. The machine acts as an artificial kidney and tries to re-establish the normal levels of ions and water in their bodies.

Quick Facts

- **When your urinary bladder is full, it is large enough to be noticeable, and when the urinary bladder is almost half full, the person discharges urine.**
- **Approximately 75 percent of human waste is made of water.**
- **The average person expels flatulence 14 times each day.**
- **Skin is not a part of the excretory system.**
- **Bladder cancer forms when cells lining the urinary bladder are abnormal.**
- **Kidney stones can move through your body.**
- **Kidney cancer forms when cells in the tissues of the kidney are abnormal.**

- Kidney stones can be of the size of golf balls.
- Most common symptom of kidney cancer is blood in the urine.
- The colour of the urine is pale straw or amber.
- Water forms about 95 percent of the urine.
- Nephrones are urine-forming structures of the kidneys.

Chapter - 3

THE DIGESTIVE SYSTEM

The human digestive system is responsible for breaking down the food we consume into smaller molecules that are usable by the body to obtain *energy and nutrition*. A very complex process, digestion consists of various organs, such as *intestines, stomach*, etc., most of which are *tubular* in shape.

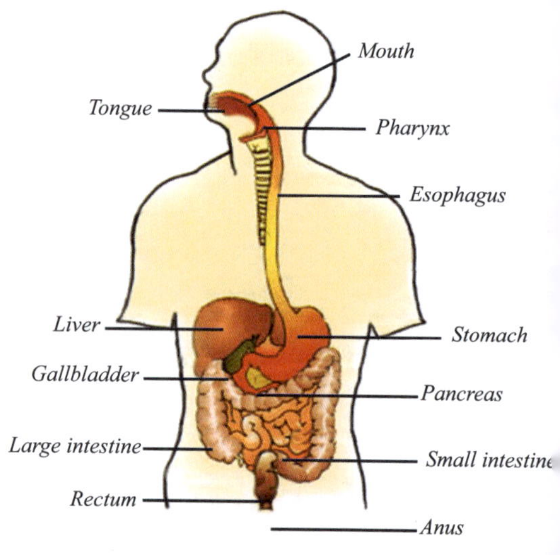

Digestive System

The process of digestion starts from the *mouth*. In the mouth, food is partially broken down by chewing with the help of certain chemical action of the *salivary enzymes*. These enzymes are produced by the *salivary glands* and are responsible for breaking down starches into smaller molecules.

From the mouth, the chewed and swallowed food travels to the stomach through the *esophagus*, which is a long tube that runs from the mouth to the stomach. The esophagus uses coordinated, wave-like muscle movements to move food from the throat to the stomach. This rhythmic movement of the esophagus is called the *peristaltic*

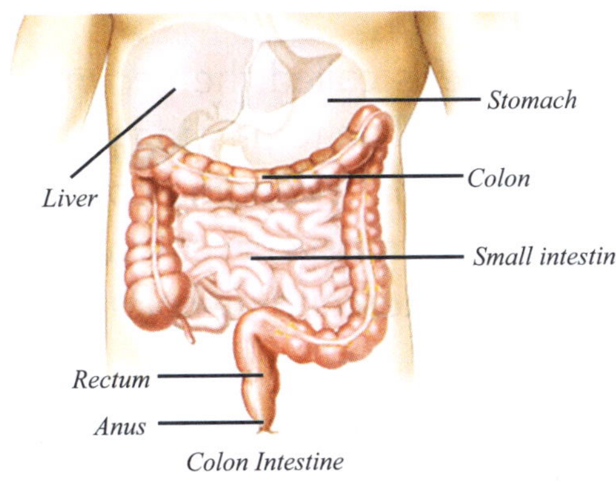

Colon Intestine

movement. The movement of this muscle gives us the ability to eat or drink even when we're upside-down!

Once the food reaches the stomach which is a huge, sack-like organ, the food is churned and gets soaked in a very strong acid, called the *gastric acid*, which is basically the *Hydrochloric acid*. Food in the stomach that is partly digested and mixed with stomach acids is called the *chyme*.

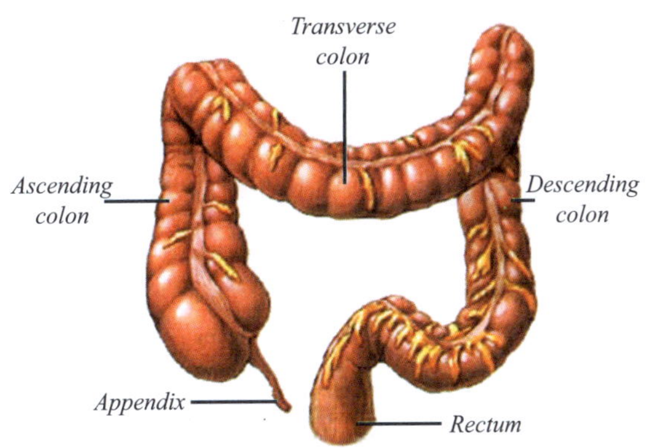

Large Intestine

The food then travels to the small intestine. Here, it enters the *duodenum*, which is the first part of the small intestine. It then goes on to the *jejunum* and then the *ileum*, which are the final parts of the small intestine. At this stage, the bile juice produced in the liver and the pancreatic enzymes, along with other digestive enzymes produced by the inner wall of the small intestine assist in further breakdown of the food.

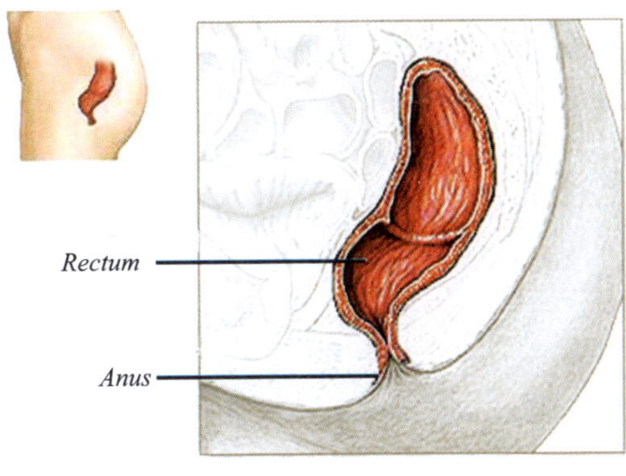

Rectum and Anus

After the small intestine, the food travels to the large intestine. Here, some of the water and chemicals like sodium are filtered out from the food. Various microbes (bacteria like Bacteroides, Escherichia coli, and Klebsiella) present in the large intestine also play a role in the digestion process. The first part of the large intestine is called the *cecum* or *caecum*, to which the *appendix* is connected. The remaining part of food then moves in an upward direction to the *ascending colon*. It then travels across the abdomen, through the transverse colon, goes back down the other side of the body in the *descending colon*, and then through the *sigmoid colon*.

The process of digestion then ends as the solid waste, which is stored in the *rectum*, is ejected out through the *anus*.

Quick Facts

- **One can live without one's appendix.**
- **The food stays in our colon for 10 hours or for several days.**
- **We eat about 500kg of food per year and about 1.7 litres of saliva is produced each day.**
- **Our stomach can hold up to 1.5 litres of water or liquid material.**
- **One of the main functions of the mouth is to either cool or warm food to a neutral temperature acceptable for the rest of the digestive tract.**
- **An adult's stomach can hold approximately 1 litre of food, and it can expand four times its normal volume.**
- **The small intestine is at least 20 feet long.**
- **The large intestine is much shorter than the small Intestine. It is approximately 5 feet long. The designation of 'small' and 'large' has to do with the width of the tube.**

Chapter - 4

THE NERVOUS SYSTEM

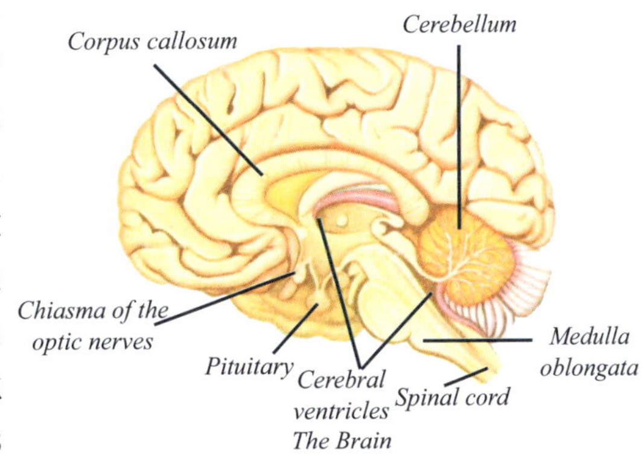

The Brain

The brain is central organ that controls all bodily functions. The nervous system is like a network that sends messages back and forth from the brain to different parts of the body. It does this via the spinal cord, which runs from the brain down through the back and contains threadlike nerves that are connected to every organ and the part of body.

When a message comes into the brain from anywhere in the body, the brain tells the body how to react. For example, if you accidentally touch a hot stove, the nerves in your skin shoot a message of pain to your brain. The brain then sends a message back telling the muscles in your hand to pull away. All this happens within a very short period of time.

The nervous system is divided into two kinds of systems:

The Central Nervous System

The Central Nervous System (CNS) is the processing centre for the nervous system. It receives information from and sends information to the Peripheral Nervous System. The two main organs of the CNS are the **brain** and the **spinal cord**. The human brain weighs just **3 pounds**. It has many folds and grooves which provide it with additional surface area necessary for storing all of important information of the body.

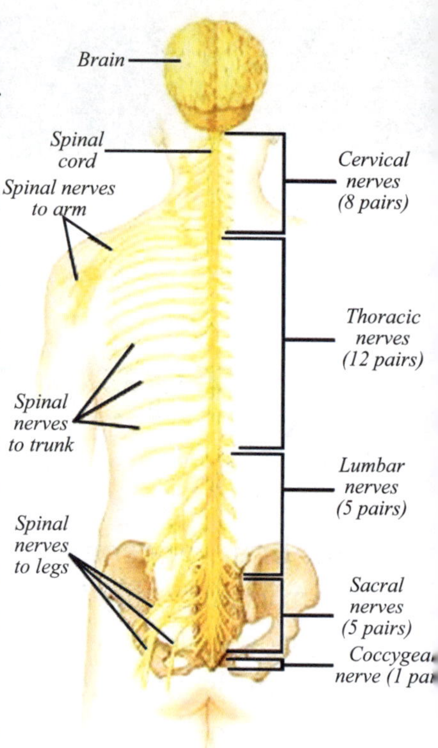

The **spinal cord** is a long bundle of nerve tissues about 18 inches long and ¾ inch thick. It extends from the lower part of the brain down through the spine. The spinal cord is protected by a set of ring-shaped bones called the **vertebrae**.

They're cushioned by layers of membranes called the *meninges* and a special fluid called the **cerebrospinal fluid**. This fluid helps to protect nerve tissues, keep it healthy, and remove the waste products.

Central Nervous System

The Peripheral Nervous System

Various nerves branch out from the spinal cord to the entire body. These are together called the Peripheral Nervous System.

The functioning of the nervous system depends on tiny cells called the **neurons**. The brain has a huge number of neurons, and all of them have specialised jobs. All the neurons send information and messages to each other through a *complex electrochemical process* that creates connections which affect the way our body functions. There are mainly two kinds of neurons, the **sensory** and the **motor neurons**.

The Sensory Neurons send information from the Sensory Receptors (e.g., in skin, eyes, nose, tongue, ears) towards the Central Nervous System.

The Motor Neurons send information from the central nervous system to the muscles or glands.

The Peripheral Nervous System is connected with various organs and structures of the body through **cranial nerves** and **spinal nerves**. There are *12 pairs of cranial nerves* in the brain that have connections in the head and upper body, and *31 pairs of spinal nerves* are connected to the rest of the body. While some cranial nerves contain only sensory neurons, most cranial nerves and all spinal nerves contain both motor and sensory neurons.

At the time of birth, the nervous system contains all the neurons we have, but all of them are not connected to each other. As you grow and learn, messages travel from one neuron to the other, thereby creating connections. For instance, a certain task may seem hard to perform in the beginning, but after you get used to, it becomes a part of you. This happens because a connection has now been made between the neurons.

Divisions of Peripheral Nervous System

- **Sensory Nervous System:** It sends information to the Central Nervous System (CNS) from our internal body organs or from the external stimuli.
- **Motor Nervous System:** This carries information from the CNS to different organs, muscles and glands.
- **Somatic Nervous System:** It controls the skeletal muscles as well as the external sensory organs, such as eyes, nose, ears.
- **Autonomic Nervous System:** This controls involuntary muscles, such as smooth and cardiac muscles.

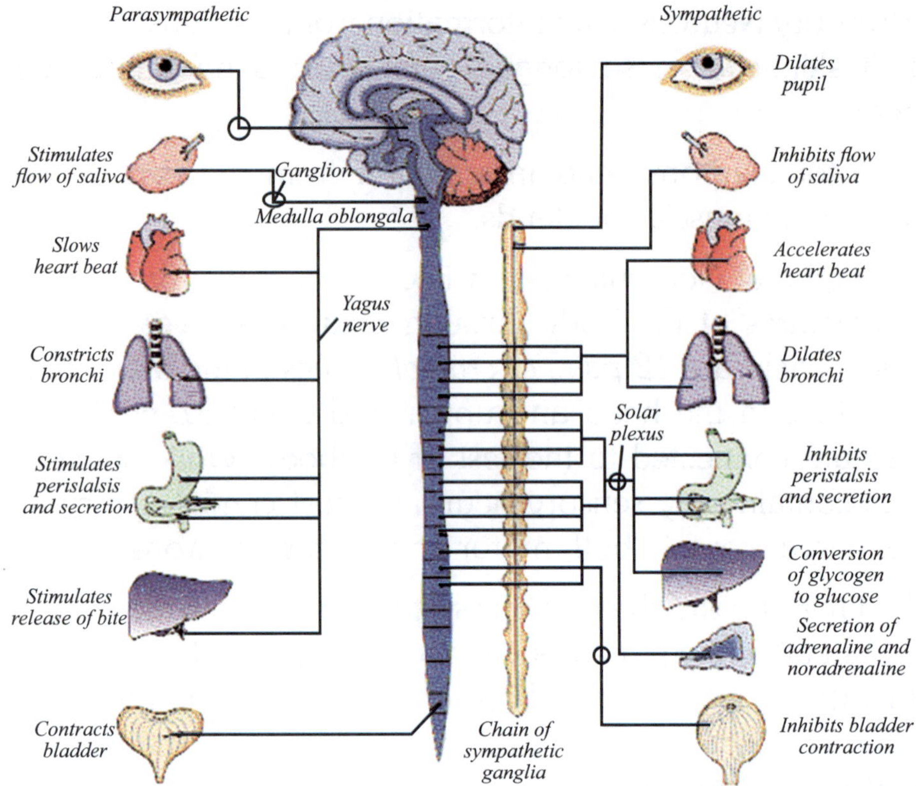

Peripheral Nervous System

- **Sympathetic System:** It controls activities that require high amounts of energy. It prepares the body for any kind of sudden stress or tension.
- **Parasympathetic System:** It controls activities that conserve the body's energy and help it to rest.

Quick Facts

- **The human brain cell can hold five times as much information as the Encyclopedia Britannica.**
- **Nerve impulses to and from the brain travel as fast as 170 miles per hour.**

- In humans, the right side of the brain controls the left side of the body, while the left side of the brain controls the right side.
- There are millions of nerve cells in the human body. This number even exceeds the number of stars in the Milky Way.
  - The diameter of the neurons can range between 4 to 100 microns.
  - In a child developing inside the womb, neurons grow at the rate of 250,000 neurons per minute.
  - By the time of its birth, the baby's brain consists of around 10 million nerve cells or neurons.
  - The weight of the brain in average adult males is about 1375 grams, while in females, it is around1275 grams, and as we grow older, the brain loses a gram each year.
  - At a given point of time, only 4 percent of the cells in the brain are active, the rest are kept in reserve.

Chapter - 5

THE HEART AND THE CIRCULATORY SYSTEM

The heart is actually a muscle, which is located to the left of the middle of the chest. The size of the heart is about the same size of a fist.

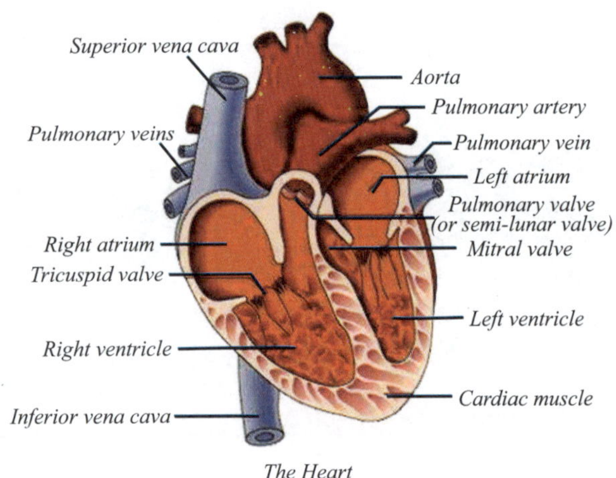

The Heart

The heart is a very special kind of muscle. Its job is to send blood all over the body. The heart and the circulatory system (also called the **cardiovascular system**) make up the network that delivers blood to the body tissues. With each heartbeat, blood is sent throughout our bodies, carrying oxygen and nutrients to all of our cells and also carrying away waste products. Our heart is like a **pump**. There are two sides of the heart. The left side receives blood from the lungs and pumps it to the rest of the body. The right side does the opposite. It receives blood from the various organs of the body and pumps it to the lungs. The heart fills with blood before each beat. Then its muscles contract to squirt the blood ahead.

Parts of the Heart

The heart is made of four different blood-filled areas called chambers. There are two chambers on each side of the heart. The top two chambers are called **atria**. The atria fill with the blood returning to the heart from the body and the lungs. The heart has a left atrium and a *right atrium*. The bottom two chambers are called *ventricles*. The heart has a *left ventricle* and a *right ventricle*. Their job is to send blood to the body and the lungs. Running down the middle of the heart is a thick wall of muscle called the *septum*. Its job is to separate left and right side of the heart.

How the Circulatory System Works

The *atria* and the *ventricles* work together- the atria fill with blood, and then send it to the ventricles. The ventricles then squeeze, pumping blood out of the heart.

While the ventricles are squeezing, the atria refill and get ready for the next contraction.

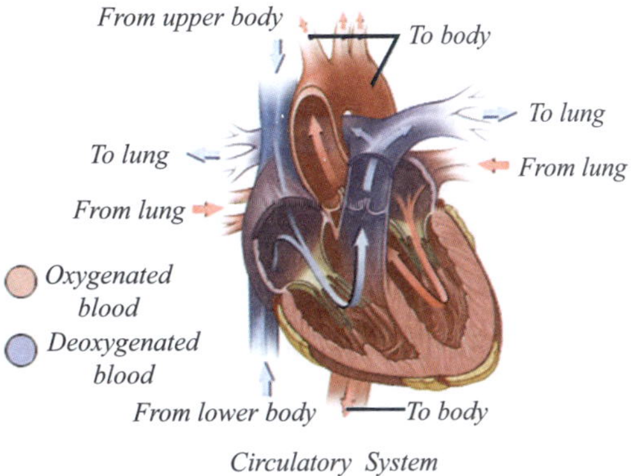

Circulatory System

Blood circulates through *four valves inside the heart*. Two of the heart valves are *mitral valves* and the other two are *tricuspid valves*. They let blood flow from the atria to the ventricles. The other two are called the *aortic valve* and the *pulmonary valve*, and they're in charge of controlling the flow as the blood leaves the heart. These valves work to keep the blood flowing forward. They open up to let the blood move ahead, and then they close quickly to keep the blood from flowing backward.

The blood moves around in our body through a series of tubes called the **arteries** and **veins**, which are collectively called *blood vessels*. These blood vessels are attached to the heart. The blood vessels that carry blood away from the heart are called the arteries. The ones that carry blood back to the heart are called the veins. This whole system is called the **circulatory system**, and this is our body's lifeline.

The movement of the blood through the heart and around the body is called circulation. The heart takes *less than 60 seconds* to pump blood to every cell in our body. Blood delivers oxygen to all the cells of the body. To stay alive, a person needs healthy, living cells. Without oxygen, these cells would die. If that oxygen-rich blood doesn't circulate as it should, a person could die. The left side of your heart sends that oxygen-rich blood out to the body. The body takes the oxygen out of the blood and uses it in your body's cells. When the cells use the oxygen, they make carbon dioxide and other waste products that get carried away by the blood.

The returning blood enters the right side of the heart. The right ventricle pumps the blood to the lungs for a little freshening up. In the lungs, carbon dioxide is removed from the blood and sent out of the body when we **exhale**. After we **inhale**, the whole process starts again. All this happens in less than a minute.

Pulse

A way to know that the heart is working, from the outside, is to feel our pulse. We can find our pulse by lightly pressing on the skin anywhere there's a large artery running just beneath our skin. Two good places to find it are on the side of our neck and the inside of our wrist, just below the thumb. When we feel a small beat under our skin, that is when we have found our pulse. Each beat is caused by contraction of the heart. An adult normal human heart beats about **72 times per minute**.

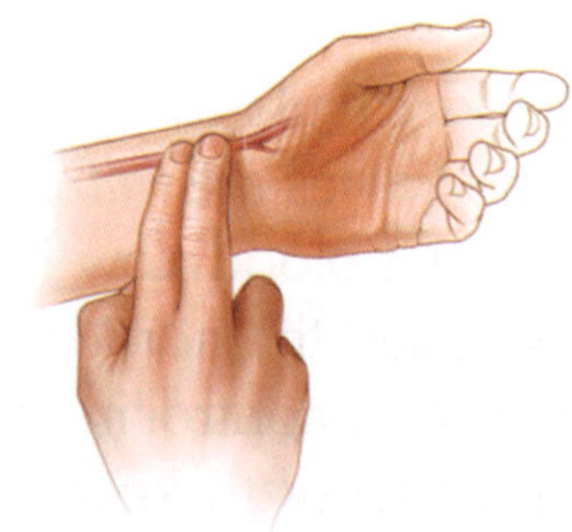

Heart Beats (Pulse)

Quick Facts

- The human heart creates enough pressure to squirt blood to about 30 feet.
- The human body is estimated to have 60,000 miles of blood vessels.
- Simple and moderately severe sunburn damages the blood vessels extensively.
- A woman's heart beats faster than a man's heart. The main reason for this is simply that on average, women tend to be smaller than men and have less mass to pump blood to.
- The aorta is the largest artery of the human body. All the arteries carry the blood out of your heart.
- Veins carry the blood back to the heart.
- If your blood vessels were strung together and measured, they would circle the globe 2 1/2 times.
- In just one to two minutes, blood circulates throughout your whole body. It brings the oxygen out and the carbon dioxide back within that short span of time, and then it repeats, and repeats and repeats your whole life.

Chapter - 6

NUTRITION

Human body is extremely complex in nature and hence, requires energy to function and nutrients to grow and repair any damage in body. These nutrients and energy come from food. Therefore, the consumption of a good balanced diet is essential.

Nutrition can be broadly categorised into three types of food – **carbohydrates, proteins** and **fats**. Apart from these major components, tiny amounts of **vitamins** and **minerals** are also required. Other key components include **water** and **fibre**. To stay in good shape, a person should eat a variety of food in adequate proportions.

The main source of energy for our body, i.e. carbohydrates can be categorised into two parts – *Complex carbohydrates* and *Sweet-tasting sugars*.

- **Complex Carbohydrates:** The main complex carbohydrate in our body is starch. Pastas, cereals, bread, rice, potatoes, etc. are rich in starch. Such foods, containing complex carbohydrates should constitute at least half of our diet, as during digestion, this starch is broken up into sugar glucose, which is the main source of energy for the body.

- **Sugars:** Foods containing this form of carbohydrates should be eaten sparingly as they contain a lot of added sugar. Sweets, cakes, biscuits contain sugar. These foods give the body a sudden energy burst rather than a constant stream. These foods also cause the problem of weight gain.

- **Proteins and Dairy Products:** Proteins and dairy products ensure the growth and development of the body. They also help in repairing the damaged parts of our system. Foods rich in proteins are fish, pulses, eggs, meat, nuts, etc. Dairy products enable healthy bone growth. For example, milk and cheese supply bone-building mineral, called the calcium. These foods should constitute at least 15% of our diet.

- **Fats and Oils:** Fats and oils are responsible for providing vitamins that are essential for smooth functioning of our body. However, they should be consumed in moderation as animal foods contain saturated fatty acids which can clog

the arteries. However, plant oils, such as olive oil, containing unsaturated fatty acids are good for health.

- **Fruits and Vegetables:** These are the most essential parts of a diet and should be consumed in abundance. Fruits are a great source of fibre, water and minerals that give us energy and replenish our bodies. They also supply antioxidants which reduce the possibility of contracting diseases. Vegetables are also rich in fibre, and hence are a vital part of a balanced diet.

Quick Facts

- **We can survive for months without food but only a few days without water.**
- **One tires easily due to lack of iron in the body.**
- **Water helps to regulate the temperature of body. Water rids the body of waste materials and transports vital nutrients to the cells.**
- **Plants can manufacture most of the nutrients that they need to function but human beings cannot, humans must obtain nutrients by eating plants and animals.**

Chapter - 7

IMMUNITY

The immune system of our body is like a *defence system* that protects us from all the foreign particles that enter it. It is a collection of molecules, cells and organs whose complex interactions form an efficient system that is usually able to protect an individual from both foreign invaders and its own internal cells. This way our body stays protected from infections and diseases.

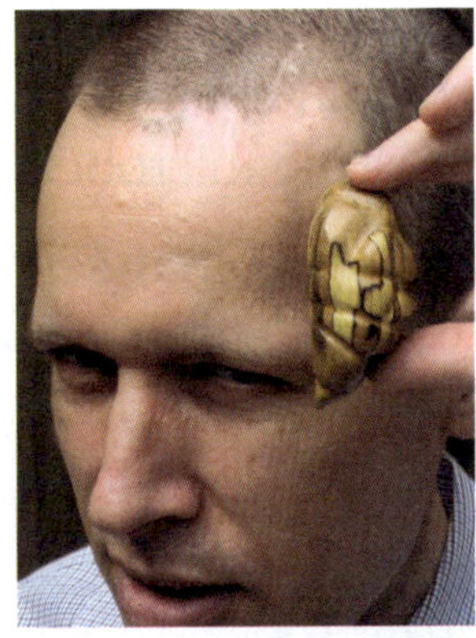

Brain Tumour

The combination mentioned above has emerged after millions of years of evolution, which has targeted those species that are worthy of preventing their destruction from the attack of **micro-organisms** or **tumours**.

A very peculiar fact about the human immunity is that it works the most when it doesn't have to work at all, meaning at the time the body is not contracted by diseases. Therefore, if the infectious *bacteria* or *viruses* are unable to enter an individual's body, no further immune response will be needed. Hence, the person remains healthy.

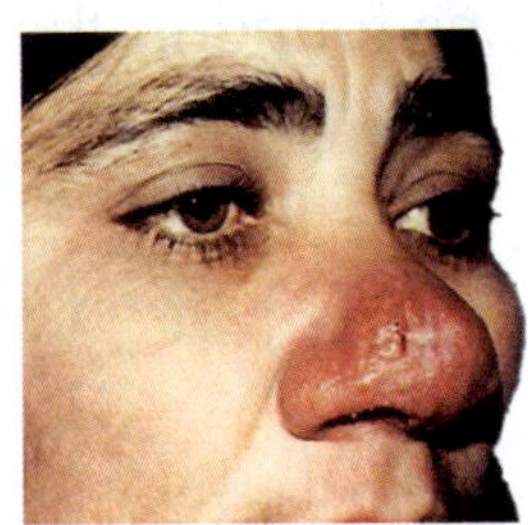

It is important to note that two other body parts that are not usually associated with the immune system also serve vital functions. These are the **Skin** and the **Mucosa**. While it seems elementary, the importance of skin in resisting infection cannot be overlooked. It is the skin which stops most of micro-organisms from entering the body, hence, protecting it against **diseases**. To appreciate its importance, it is important to consider the relative frequency of wounds or rashes forming on healthy skin, as compared to where the skin has been infected.

The other important feature is the Mucosa. It is the tissue which covers our eyes, alimentary canal, urinary and genital tracts. If the frequency of infections at these areas is high, it gets difficult for the tissue to resist them. It is lesser efficient than the skin in this job as it is easier to penetrate this tissue.

Tears and saliva, as well as other mucus secretions perform the job of washing away many potential attackers, and many also contain chemical elements which are effective in killing microbes.

The cells that serve the Immune system are known as the **B-Cells** and the **T-Cells**. The T-Cells act to destroy the infected or cancerous cells, and also coordinate all the acquired immune responses. The T-Cell immunity is generally called the *cellular immunity*.

On the other hand, the B-Cells provide humoral immunity as it consists of dissolved proteins found in the 'Humors' (Blood).

Quick Facts

- Increasing stress leads to decreasing immunity.
- We get an allergy when the immune system responds to a harmless substance.
- Coughing and sneezing are part of the natural immunity system where the body is trying to eject pathogens and irritants from the respiratory system.
- Saliva, tears and breast milk contain antibacterial enzymes to help fight off harmful bacteria.
- One of the first responses to infection by the immune system is inflammation.
- Fever can sometimes help the immune system fight off infection because certain pathogens are unable to tolerate higher temperatures.
- The lungs and intestines secrete mucus, which can trap micro-organisms, preventing them from entering the bloodstream and tissues.
- The gastric acid produced by the stomach not only aids in digestion but is also a chemical barrier that destroys many forms of ingested pathogens.

Part - III

THE EXTERNAL ORGANS

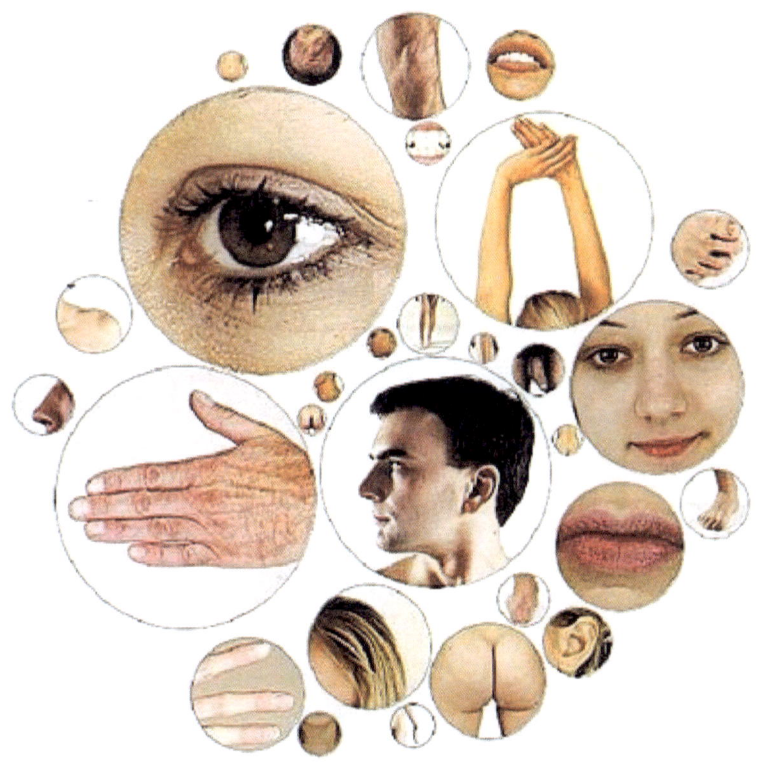

Chapter - 1

MOUTH

The mouth plays a key role in the **digestive system**. The mouth, especially the teeth, lips, and tongue, is essential for speech. The tongue, which allows us to taste, also helps form words when we speak. The lips that line the outside of the mouth both help hold food in while we chew and pronounce words when we talk.

Along with the lips and tongue, the teeth help to form words by controlling air flow out of the mouth. The tongue strikes the teeth as certain sounds are made.

The hardest substances in the body, the teeth are also necessary for *chewing*, the process by which we tear, cut, and grind food for swallowing. Chewing allows enzymes and lubricants release in the mouth to further digest food.

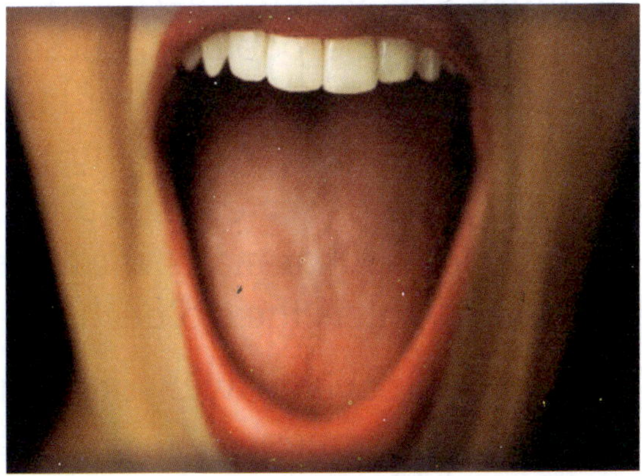

Mouth

Basic Anatomy

The mouth is the entrance to the digestive tract, and is lined with *mucus membranes*. The roof of the mouth is called the *palate*. The front part consists of a bony portion called the *hard palate*, with a fleshy rear part called the *soft palate*. The hard palate divides the mouth and the nasal passages above. The soft palate forms a curtain between the mouth and the throat, or pharynx, to the rear. The soft palate contains the *uvula*, the dangling flesh at the back of the mouth. The *tonsils* are located on either side of the uvula. They hold up the opening to the pharynx.

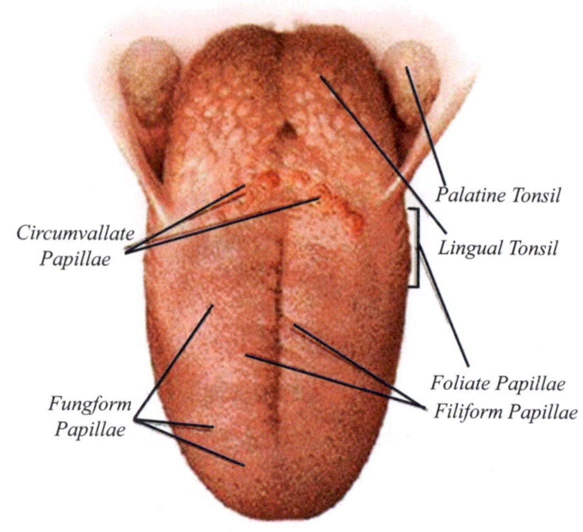

Part of the Tongue

A bundle of muscles extends from the floor of the mouth to form the tongue. The upper surface of the tongue is covered with tiny bumps called the *papillae*. These contain tiny pores that are our *taste buds*. Four main kinds of taste buds are found on the tongue — those that sense sweet, salty, sour, and bitter tastes. Three pairs of salivary glands secrete saliva, which contains a digestive enzyme called *amylase* that starts the breakdown of carbohydrates even before food enters the stomach.

The lips are covered with skin on the outside and with slippery mucous membranes on the inside of the mouth. The major lip muscle, called the *orbicularis oris*, allows for the lips' mobility. The reddish tint of the lips comes from the underlying blood vessels. The inside portion of both the lips is connected to the *gums*.

There are several types of teeth. **Incisors** are squarish, sharp-edged teeth in the front of the mouth. There are four on the bottom and four on the top. On either side of the incisors are the sharp canines. Behind the **canines** are the **premolars**, or **bicuspids**. There are two sets in each jaw. The molars, situated behind the premolars, have points and grooves. There are 12 molars — three sets in each jaw called the first, second, and the third molars.

Human teeth are made up of four different types of tissue: *pulp, dentin, enamel, and cementum*. The pulp is the innermost portion of the tooth and consists of the connective tissue, nerves and blood vessels, which nourish the tooth. **Dentin** surrounds the pulp. It is a hard yellow substance, and makes up most of the tooth and is as hard as the bone. It's the dentin that gives teeth their yellowish tint. **Enamel**, the hardest tissue in the body, covers the dentin and forms the outermost layer of the crown. It enables the tooth to withstand the pressure of chewing and protects it from harmful bacteria. It also helps to withstand changes in the temperature from hot and cold foods. Both the dentin and pulp extend into the roots of the teeth. A bony layer of cementum covers the outside of the root, under the gum line, and holds the tooth in place within the jawbone. **Cementum** is also as hard as the bone.

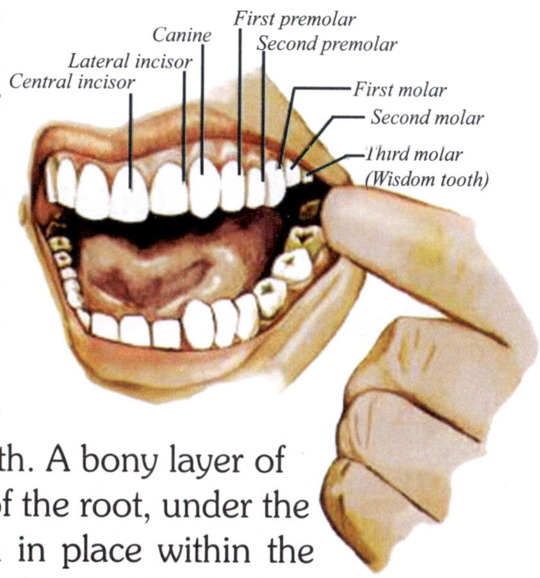

Types of Teeth

What do the mouth and teeth do?

The first step of digestion involves the mouth and teeth. Food enters the mouth and is immediately broken down into smaller pieces by our teeth. Each type of tooth serves a different function in the chewing process. **Incisors** cut foods when you bite into them. The sharper and longer **canines** tear food. The **premolars**, which are flatter than the canines, grind and mash food. **Molars**, with their points and grooves, are responsible for the most vigorous chewing. The tongue helps to push the food up against our teeth.While chewing, the salivary glands secrete saliva, which moistens the food and helps break it down even more. Saliva makes it easier to chew and swallow foods and it contains enzymes that aid in the digestion.

Once food has been converted into a soft, moist mass, it's pushed into the throat (or pharynx) at the back of the mouth and is swallowed. When we swallow, the soft palate closes off the nasal passages from the throat to prevent food from entering the nose.

Proper dental care including a good diet, frequent cleaning of the teeth after eating, and regular dental checkups, all these are essential in maintaining healthy teeth and avoiding tooth decay and gum diseases.

Quick Facts

- **If saliva cannot dissolve something, you cannot taste it.**
- **The tooth is the only part of the human body that can't repair itself.**
- **Throughout your life, the amount of saliva you have could fill two swimming pools.**
- **If your mouth was completely dry, you would not be able to distinguish the taste of anything.**
- **Humans have unique tongue prints, just like fingerprints.**
- **The tongue is the strongest muscle in the body.**

Chapter - 2

EARS

We hear many different sounds all around us. The parts of body that help us to hear are the ears.

The ears collect sounds, process them, and send sound signals to our brain. Also, our ears help us keep our balance, which means that they help us in standing straight and not falling down.

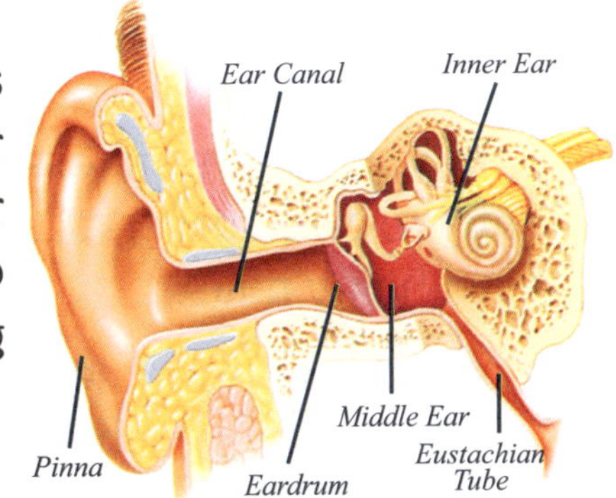

Parts of Human Ear

Parts of the Ear

The ear has three different sections:

- **Outer Ear:** This part is also called the pinna or auricle. This is the part of the ear that can be seen. The outer ear hears and collects sounds. The outer ear also includes the ear canal, the place where the earwax is produced. Earwax protects the ear canal. It contains chemicals that fight infections that may hurt the skin in the canal. It also collects dirt to help keep the ear canal clean.
- **Middle Ear:** Sound waves, after entering the ear, travel through the ear canal to the middle ear. The middle ear's

main job is to take these sound waves and turn them into vibrations, which are then sent to the inner ear. To do this, it needs the eardrum, a thin piece of skin which is stretched tight to seem like a drum. When sound waves reach the ear drum, it vibrates. The sound then moves to the ossicles, which are three tiny bones in our ear. These are called:

- **Hammer:** which is attached to the ear drum
- **Anvil:** which is attached to the hammer
- **Stirrup:** which is attached to the anvil, and is also the smallest bone in the body. These bones help the sound waves in moving to the inner ear.
- **Inner Ear:** Sounds enter the inner ear in the form of vibrations, and from there enter the cochlea which is a small, curled tube. The cochlea is filled with liquid, which is set into motion when the ossicles vibrate. The cochlea is lined with tiny cells covered with tiny hairs.
- **The Cochlea:** The sounds move the hair on the cells, creating nerve signals for the brain.

The brain then recognises various sounds that it receives.

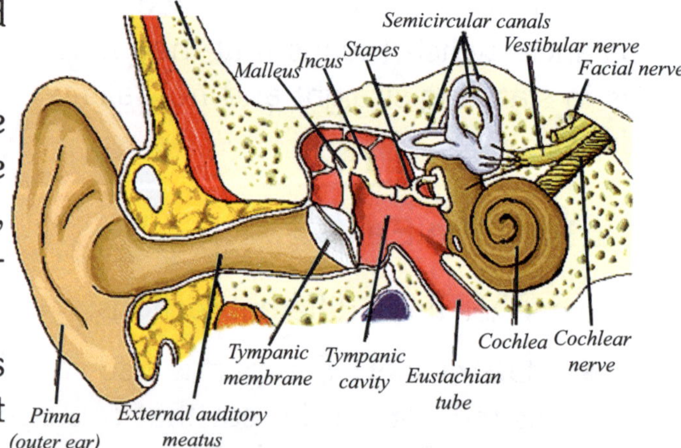

The Internal Structure of Human Ear

Maintaining Balance

Ears also help us maintain our balance. In the inner ear, there are three small loops above the cochlea called **semicircular canals**. They are filled with liquid and have tiny microscopic hair, just like cochlea. When we move our heads, the liquid moves too. The liquid moves tiny hairs, which send a nerve message to the brain about the position of our heads. Within a second, the brain sends a message to the right muscles so that we can keep our balance.

Quick Facts

- Earwax production is necessary for good ear health.
- After eating too much, your hearing is less sharp.
- Your ears secrete more earwax when you are afraid than when you aren't.
- The smallest bone in your body, the stirrup, is in your ears.

Chapter - 3

EYES

The eyes are one of the most spectacular parts of the body because they let us view the world all around us. Except for when we are sleeping, our eyes are always working. They take in information from what we see in the world, and then send that information to our brain so that the brain knows what is happening around us.

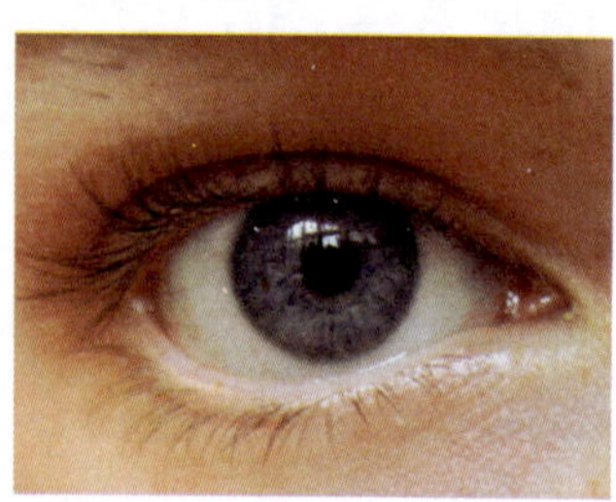

The Human Eye

Parts and Functions of the Eye

The eye rests in a hollow area called the **eye socket**, in the skull. The eyelid covers and protects the front part of the eyes. It also keeps the eye clean and moist by opening and closing several times. This action is called *blinking*. The eyelid also has amazing reflexes, in order to protect the eye. When we step into bright light, our eyelids instantly close to protect the eyes before they can adjust themselves to the light.

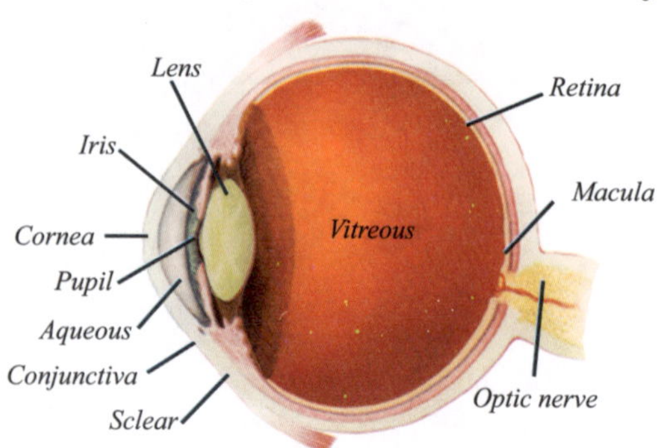

Parts of the Human Eye

The *eyelashes* are the hair that grow on the top and bottom of the *eyelid* and protect the *eyes* by keeping dust and other unwanted objects from entering the *eyes*.

The white part of the *eyeball* is called **sclera**. It is made up of a tough material, and is like an outer coat of the *eyeball*. The pink and red threads that can be seen are **blood vessels**, and provide blood to the sclera.

The **cornea** is a transparent part which sits in front of the coloured part of the *eye*. The cornea helps the *eye* focus as light makes its way through. It is a very important part of the *eye*, and gives a clear and transparent view of the world around us.

The **iris**, the **pupil** and the **anterior chamber** lie behind the *cornea*. The iris is the coloured part of the *eye*. When we say that a person has brown *eyes*, we are actually referring to his/her iris. The iris has attached muscles that change its shape. These allow the iris to control the amount of light that enters the pupil.

The pupil is situated in the centre of the iris, and is like an opening through which light enters the *eye*. Pupils get smaller when a light is shone near them, and grow bigger when the light is dimmed or gone.

The anterior chamber is the space between the *iris* and the *cornea*. It is filled with a special transparent fluid that nourishes the *eye* and keeps it healthy.

After light enters the pupil, it reaches the *lens*. The lens is situated behind the iris and is clear and colourless.

The lens then focusses light rays to the back of the *eyeball*, that is, to the retina. The retina has millions of cells that are sensitive to light. The **retina** changes the *light into nerve signals* and sends them to the brain so that the brain can understand what the *eye* is saying.

The *vitreous site behind the retina* is the biggest part of the *eye*. It gives the eye its shape. It's filled with clear and jelly-like material called the *vitreous humour*. After light passes through the lens, it shines through the vitreous humour to the back of the eye.

Rods and Cones

The retina uses *rods* and *cones* to process light. Rods see in black and white, and shades of grey. They tell us the form and shape of anything that we see. Rods don't know the difference between colours. But they are super-sensitive, and help us see in the dark. Cones sense colour, and unlike rods, are mostly helpful in normal or bright light. There are three types of cones, each of which is sensitive to the three primary colours, that is, red, green and blue. This allows one to see different ranges of colour. When they work together, these cones can sense a combination of light waves that enable us to see many colours.

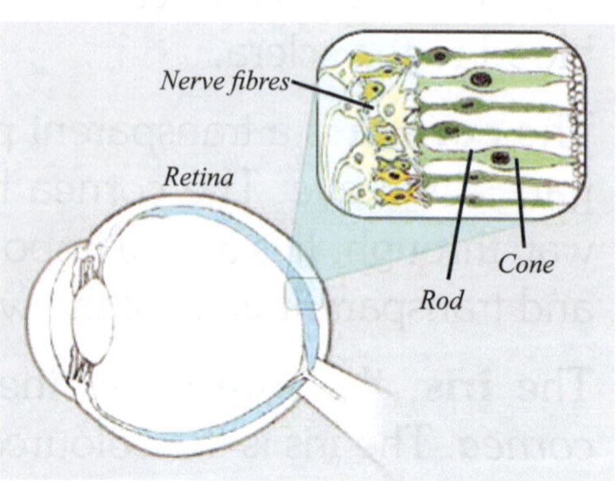

Internal Structure of an Eye

The rods and cones change the colours and shapes into *nerve messages*. These messages are then carried by the optic nerve to the brain. When we see an image, our eyes inform our brain about what they saw, and then the brain works to figure out what it is that the eyes see.

Lacrimal Glands (Tear glands)

The lacrimal glands are situated above the outer corner of each eye. These glands produce tears. Every time we blink, a little bit of tear fluid comes out of this gland. It helps wash away the dust, germs and anything else that might irritate the eyes. Tears also protect our eyes from drying out. Sometimes the eyes make more tear fluid to protect themselves. This can happen when we are poked in the eye, when we are in a very polluted place, or when we are cutting onions. Whenever we are sad or scared, the brain sends messages to the eyes to cry, and then the **lacrimal glands** make many **tears**.

Lacrimal Glands in the Eyes

Quick Facts

- Humans are the only animals to produce emotional tears.
- The pupils dilate both when you look at a person you love and at a person you hate. Even small noises cause the pupils of the eyes to dilate.
- Babies are always born with blue eyes because of the pigment, melanin. The melanin in a newborn's eyes often needs time after birth to be fully deposited or to be darkened by exposure to ultraviolet light, later revealing the baby's true eye colour.
- Eyes detect light and allow us to see.
- Our eyes blink over 27,397 times in a day.
- The eyeball of a human weighs approximately 28 grams.
- The cone cells in the retina detect colour while the rod cells detect low light.
- Glasses and contact lenses are worn to correct common sight conditions, such as short and long-sightedness.

Chapter - 4

JOINTS

The place where two **bones meet** is called a joint. Some joints **move** and others **don't**.

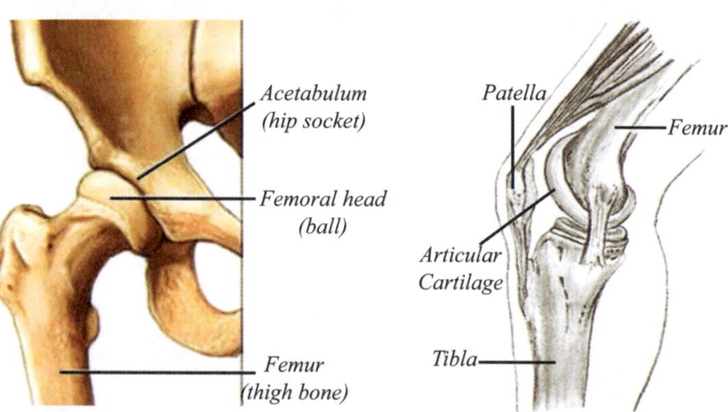

Joints of the Legs

Types of Joints

- **Fixed joints**
  these joints are fixed in place and don't move at all. Your skull has some of these joints called *sutures* which close up the bones of the skull in a young person's head.
- **Moving joints** are the ones that allow you to twist, bend and move different parts of your body. Some moving joints, like the ones in your spine, move only a little. Other joints move a lot.
  - ☆ One of the main types of moving joints is called a **hinge joint**. Your elbows and knees each have hinge joints, which let you bend and then straighten your arms and legs. These joints are like the hinges on a door. Just as most doors can only open one way, you can only

bend your arms and legs in one direction. You also have many smaller hinge joints in your fingers and toes.

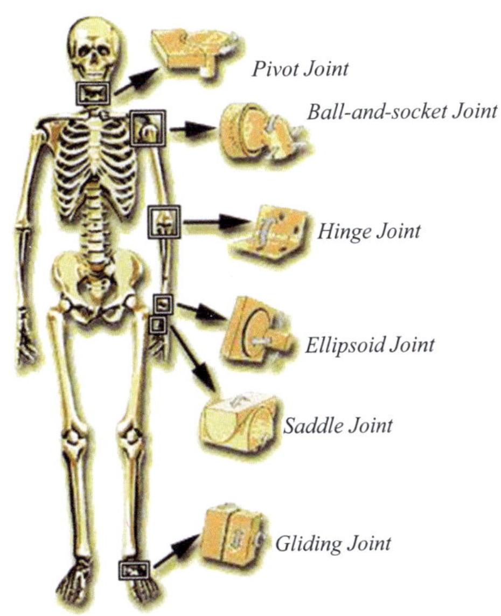

Different Types of Joints

☆ Another important type of moving joint is the **ball and socket joint**. You can find these joints at your shoulders and hips. They are made up of the round end of one bone fitting into a small cup-like area of another bone. Ball and socket joints allow for lots of movement in every direction.

Your joints come with their own special fluid called the **synovial fluid** that helps them move freely. Bones are held together at the joints by ligaments, which are like very strong rubber bands.

Quick Facts

- Humans have over 230 moveable and semi-moveable joints in their bodies.
- Some joints move and some don't. Joints in the skull don't move.
- Synovial joints are movable joints. They make up most of the joints in the body and are located mostly in the limbs, where the mobility is critical. They contain synovial fluid, which helps them to move freely.

- A coating of another fibrous tissue called cartilage covers the bone surface and keeps the bones from rubbing directly against each other.
- Tendons are made of elastic tissue and also play a key role in the functioning of joints. They connect the muscles to the bones.
- Ball and socket joints, such as hip and shoulder joints, are the most mobile type of joints. They allow you to move your arms and legs in many different directions.
- Ellipsoidal joints, such as the one at the base of the index finger, allow bending and extending.
- Gliding joints are found between flat bones that are held together by ligaments. Some bones in the wrists and ankles move by gliding against each other.
- Hinge joints are those in the knee and elbow. They enable movement similar to the way a hinged door moves.

Chapter - 5

THE SKELETAL SYSTEM

The human skeleton is a strong and flexible framework, which not only supports the shape of the body, but also produces movements when pulled by the muscles. The human body consists of **206 bones**. It is also the job of the skeleton to protect the soft, internal organs, such as the brain and lungs. It may be interesting to know that bones, which make up about 20% of the body's mass, are connected to each other at joints and are held together by strong straps of tissue, called the **ligaments**.

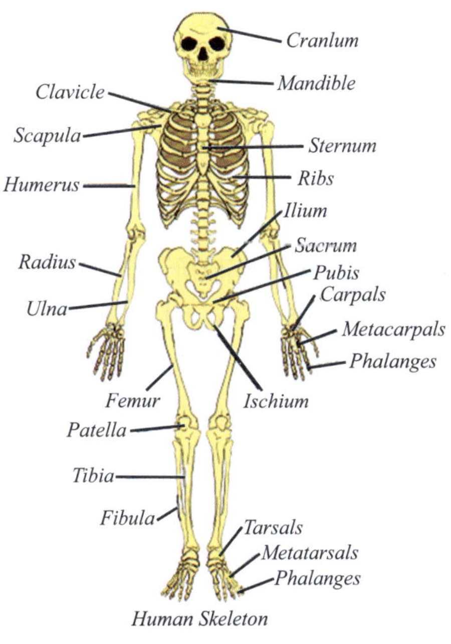

Human Skeleton

Skull

The bones in the skull are responsible for protecting the brain and provide a framework to the face. These also regulate the *facial expressions*.

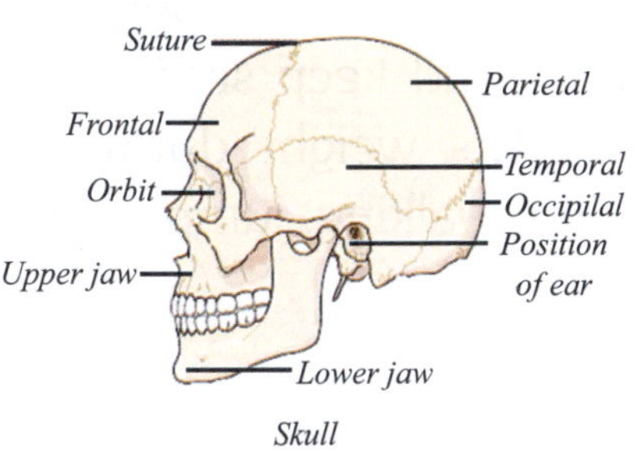

Skull

The skull consists of **22 bones**, 21 of which are locked together by **sutures**.

Chest

Chest is formed by the breastbone, ribs and part of the backbone. These bones together perform a protective cage to protect the lungs and the heart from any damage.

Forearm

Two parallel bones, the ulna and the radius together form the forearm. The ulna curves to form the elbow's point, whereas the radius forms a joint with the wrist bones.

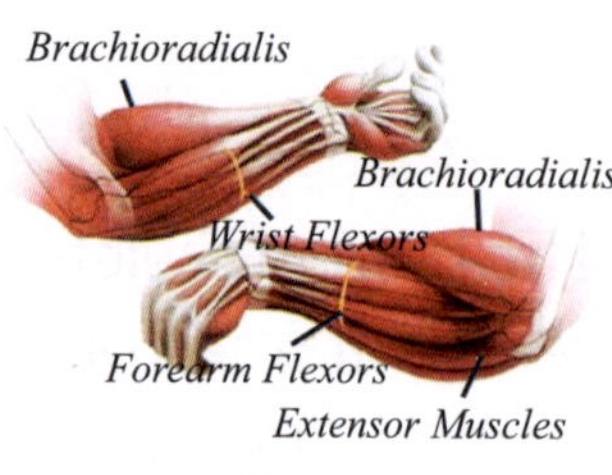

Forearm

Elbow

Elbow is the point where the upper arm and the forearm meet. The elbow acts like a door hinge, enabling the arm to bend and keep straight. The forearm can rotate the elbow, allowing the palm to face upwards or downwards.

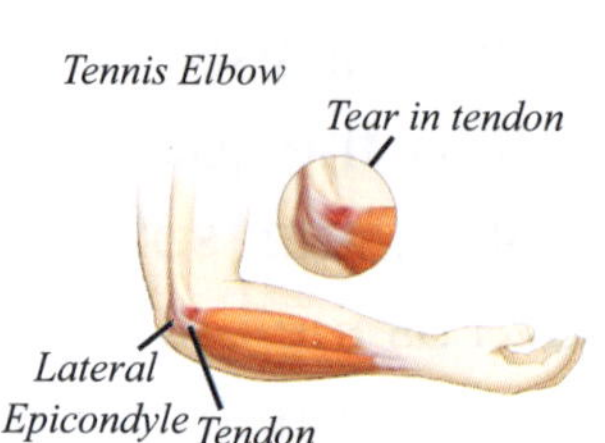

Elbow

Knee

The knee is the joint between the shin and the thigh. It is the strongest and the most complex joint of the body. It allows the leg to bend and keep straight, and supports the body's weight during activities like running, walking, jumping, etc.

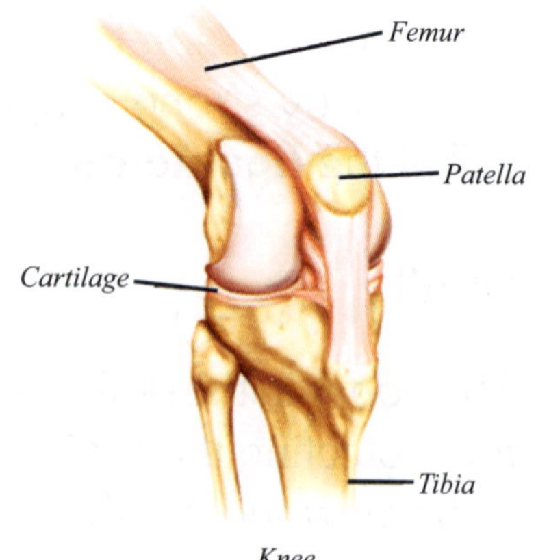

Knee

Pelvis

This is a strong, bowl shaped structure consisting of two curved hip bones. It supports abdominal organs and attaches the thigh bones to the skeleton.

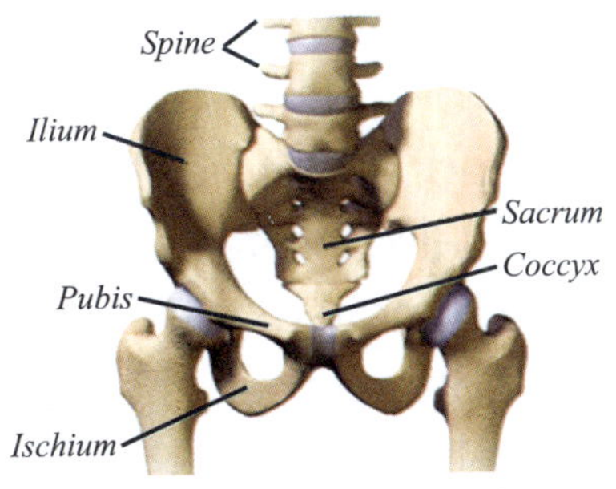

Pelvis

Hand

The hand consists of **27 bones** and many movable joints that are responsible to perform many tasks. The thumb can be rotated to touch each of the other fingers.

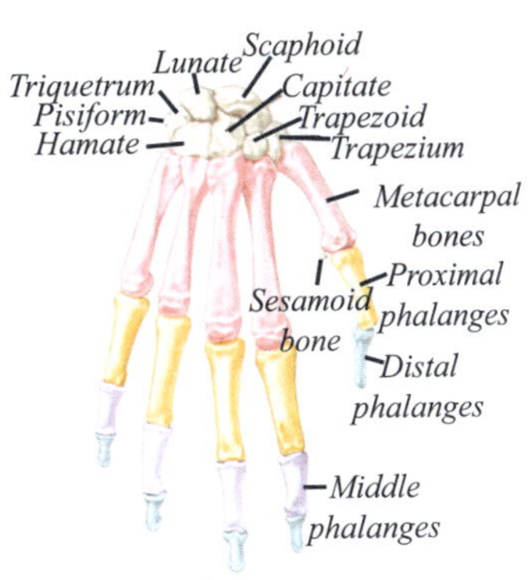

Hand

Foot

A foot consists of the **ankle**, **sole** and the **toe bones** which support and move the body's weight. They provide a flexible platform to the body.

Toes

The **phalanges** of the toes are shorter than the phalanges of the hands and not as flexible as the ones in the fingers. These help the body to propel forward.

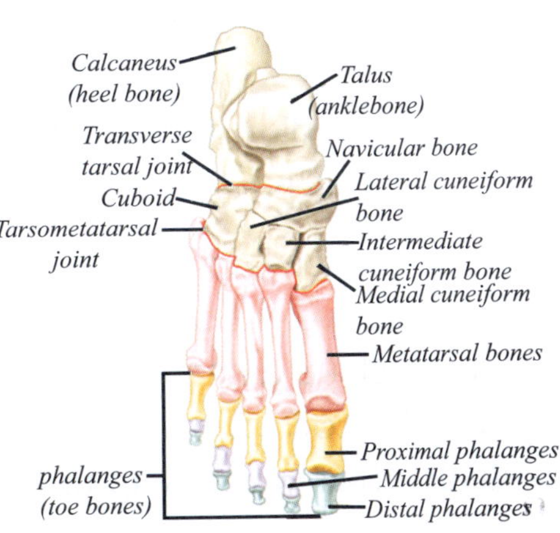

Foot and Toes

Backbone or the Spine

The spine, also known as the backbone or the **vertebral column**, consists of a long chain of **33 bones** each individually known as a *vertebra* or the *vertebrae*, which are ring-shaped. The main functions of the vertebral bones are for structure and protection of the spinal cord. The spine lets you twist and bend, and it holds your body upright. It also protects the spinal cord, a large bundle of nerves that sends information from your brain to the rest of your body.

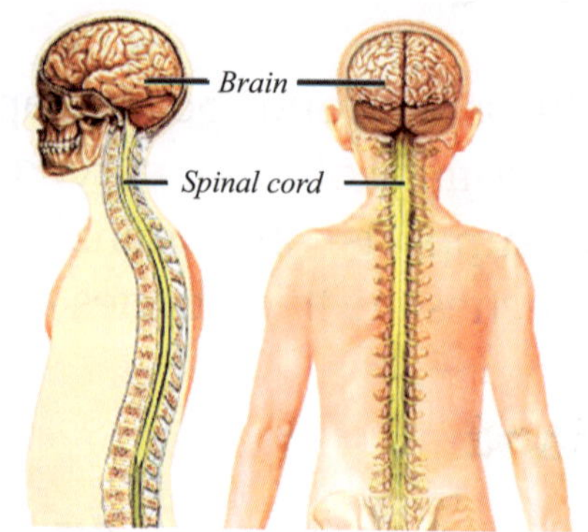

Backbone of the Spine

There are different types of vertebrae in the spine and each does a different kind of job:

- The first seven vertebrae at the top are called the **cervical vertebrae**. These bones are the back of your neck, just below your brain, and they support your head and neck.
- Below the cervical vertebrae are the **thoracic vertebrae**, and they are 12 in all. These anchor your ribs in place.
- Below the thoracic vertebrae are five **lumbar vertebrae**.
- Beneath the lumbar vertebrae is the **sacrum**, which is made up of five vertebrae that are fused together to form one single bone.
- Finally, all the way at the bottom of the spine is the **coccyx**, which is one bone made of four fused vertebrae.

The bottom sections of the spine are important when it comes to bearing weight and giving you a good centre of gravity. So when you pick up a heavy bag on an object, the lumbar vertebrae, sacrum and the coccyx give you the power. When you dance, skip and even walk, these parts help to keep you balanced.

In between each vertebra are small disks made of **cartilage**. These disks keep the vertebrae from rubbing against one another, and they also act as your spine's natural shock absorbers. When you jump in the air, the disks give your vertebrae the cushioning they need.

Quick Facts

- There are more than 20 bones in each foot.
- The only jointless bone in our body is the hyoid bone in the throat.
- Babies are born with 300 bones, but by adulthood, the number is reduced to 206.
- The hardest bone in the human body is the jawbone. A bone is actually stronger than steel.
- We are about 1 cm taller in the morning than in the evening, due to the compression of the cartilage disks.
- Most people have lower back pain. This is because the lower back bears the weight of the upper body. It also twists and bends more than the upper back.
- If you get back pain after a small movement, such as picking up a book from the floor, you could have a slipped disc or a joint problem in your spine.

Chapter - 6

THE MUSCULAR SYSTEM

Each and every movement of the human body, from a wink to a heartbeat is produced by muscles. Muscles can be categorised as skeletal muscles, smooth muscles and cardiac muscles. All muscles are made up of fibres that contract to produce a pull.

Muscles at the front of the body are responsible for our facial expressions, movement of our heads, bending of the elbow, etc.

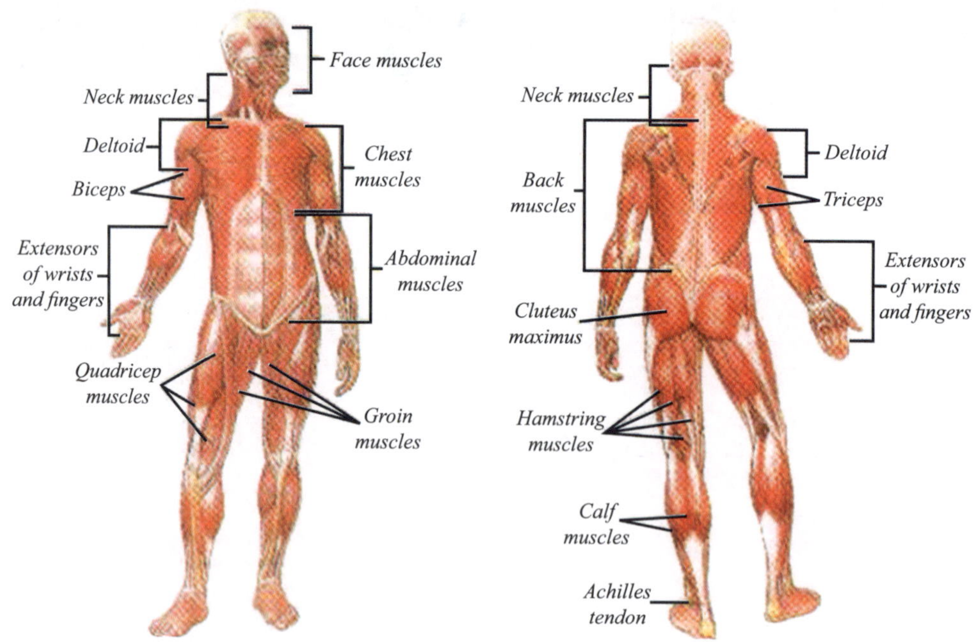

The Muscular System in Human Beings

These muscles are called the **front muscles**. **Rear muscles** of the body, on the other hand, keep the head upright, steady the shoulders, bend knees, point toes downwards, etc.

The various kinds of muscles are following:

Skeletal Muscles

These muscles are attached to the bones of the skeleton, which they pull to help us move around. Long and cylindrical fibres run parallel to each other. These can be up to 30 cm long. These fibres are bundled together to form muscles. These are attached to the bones by strong cords called the **tendons**. These muscles obey the instructions of the nervous system.

Smooth Muscles

These muscles are responsible for moving food around the intestines. These are tightly packed and layered sheets of muscle fibres and are found in hollow organs, such as the intestines, bladder, etc. in the intestine. They perform the job of pushing food around, whereas in the bladder, they help in expulsion of the urine. These muscles contract slowly and their movements cannot be controlled voluntarily.

Cardiac Muscles

Cardiac muscles are extremely important as they perform the job of keeping the heart pumping. They are found solely in the walls of the heart. These muscle fibres

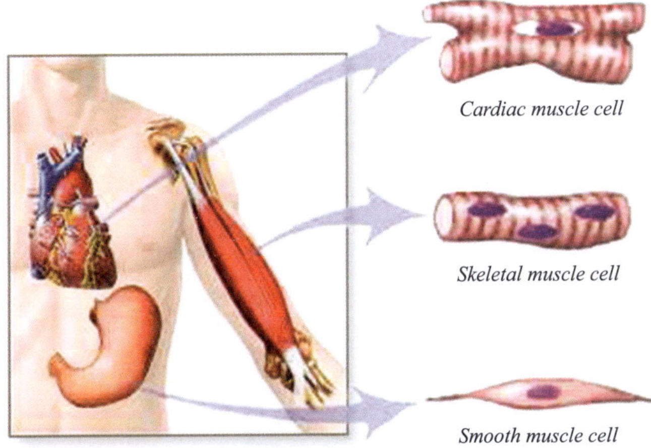

form a branching network that automatically contracts, without any stoppage. It is remarkable how these muscles never tire and constantly pump blood all around the body. However, the rate at which these muscles contract depends on the commands received by the nervous system which is a reflection of the body's demands.

Quick Facts

- **The buttock muscle is the biggest muscle of the body.**
- **The tongue alone has around 16 separate muscles.**
- **There are three types of muscles found in the human body. They are: cardiac, smooth and skeletal.**
- **Cardiac muscles are called the heart muscles.**
- **The skeletal muscles form 40% of the body weight.**
- **The smooth muscles are in the digestive tract.**
- **One can barely live without muscles.**

Chapter - 7

THE SKIN

The human skin is extremely vital to the body as it acts as a *protective overcoat* for the body. It is like a barrier between the vulnerable and delicate tissues of our body and the harsh and ever-changing conditions of the outside world. Some of the few roles played by our skin include *preventing water loss* and *invasion of germ cells*. Moreover, it also repairs itself constantly and enables us to *sense the surroundings* which we inhabit.

The skin is made up of a lot of layers. The uppermost layer of the human skin is majorly composed of dead cells. These dead cells are filled with a tough, water-proof substance called the **keratin**.

Cross-Section of the Human Skin

A section of the human skin, if analysed, reveals that it has two parts. These are the **epidermis** and the **dermis**.

While the epidermis is water resistant and germ–proof, protects us against the harmful rays of the sun, the dermis is a thicker layer,

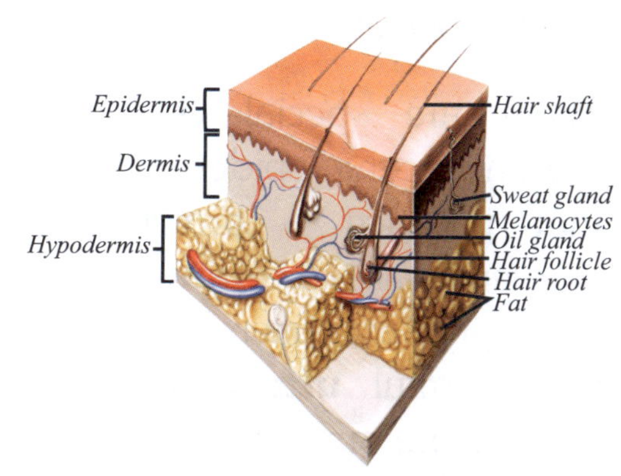

Cross-Section of the Human Skin

and contains the *blood vessels*, *sensory receptors* and the *sweat glands*.

It is interesting to know that the flat, scaly cells in the upper epidermis are constantly removed and these are replaced by the cells at the base of the epidermis, which constantly multiply to serve the purpose.

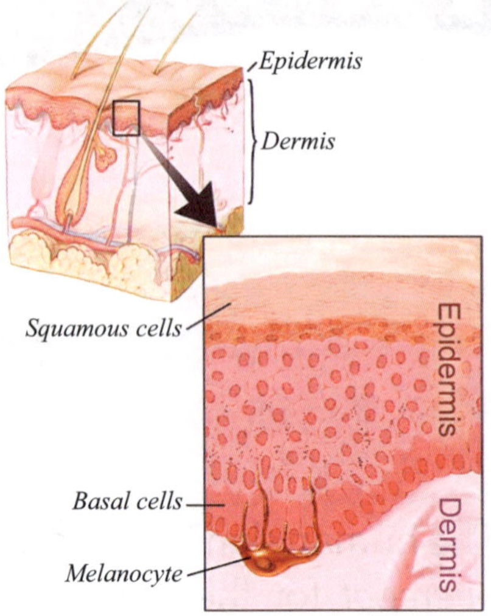

Epidermis and Dermis of Human Skin

Moreover, the epidermis contains cells that move upwards, dying, flattening and filling with **keratin**, while they do so. On the other hand, the dermis contains living cells and fibres that help the skin to stretch and recoil.

Sweat

Sweat produced by our body is a salty liquid that comes from the sweat glands in the dermis. The main purpose of sweat is to maintain a stable body temperature. In hot temperatures, the dermis releases sweat to the surface of the skin, which then gets evaporated, providing coolness to the body, hence, maintaining a stable body temperature.

Skin Colour

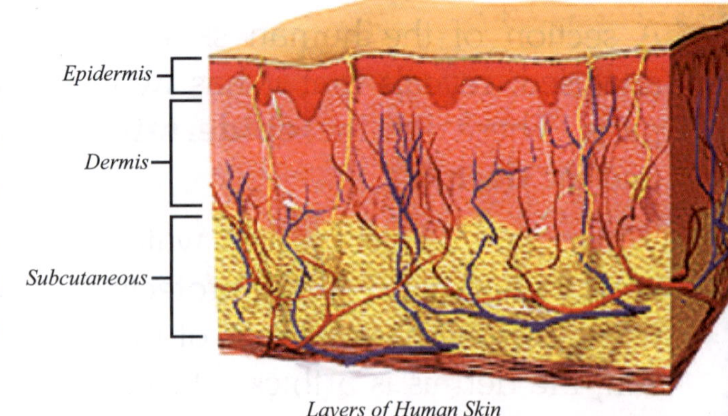

Layers of Human Skin

There are special cells present in the epidermis that produce a brown pigment called **melanin**. This pigment filters out the harmful **ultraviolet** rays of the sun, in order to protect the skin damage. It is melanin, alongwith the blood flowing through the dermis that provides the skin its colour.

Skin Colours

Quick Facts

- **Skin is the largest organ in your body and protects your body from damage. An average adult's skin spans 21 square feet, weighs nine pounds, and contains more than 11 miles of blood vessels.**
- **The skin releases as much as three gallons of sweat a day in hot weather.**
- **Vitamin D is manufactured in the skin and is essential for digesting milk.**
- **The reason our lips are red is because the skin on the lips is very thin and the blood vessels show through.**
- **Every square inch of the human body has about 19,000,000 skin cells.**
- **Skin comes in different colours – The colour of someone's skin depends on the pigment that is in their skin; people with darker pigment have darker skin. People with darker skin don't tan as much as people with paler skin, because tanning is the formation of melanin.**

Chapter - 8

THE HAIR

The entire human body is covered with hair. Some places that don't have hair include *lips*, *palms of the hands*, and *soles of the feet*.

Some of the hair on the human body is easy to see, like the hair on eyebrows, head, arms, and legs. But other hair, like that on your cheek, is almost invisible.

Depending on its location on the body, hair performs various functions. The hair on the head keeps it warm and provides cushioning to the skull. Similarly, eyelashes protect the eyes by decreasing the amount of light and dust that go into them and eyebrows protect the eyes from sweat dripping down from your forehead.

Where does the hair come from?

Whether hair is growing out of the head, arm, or ankle, it all rises out of the skin in the same way. It starts at the hair root, which is beneath the skin where cells come together

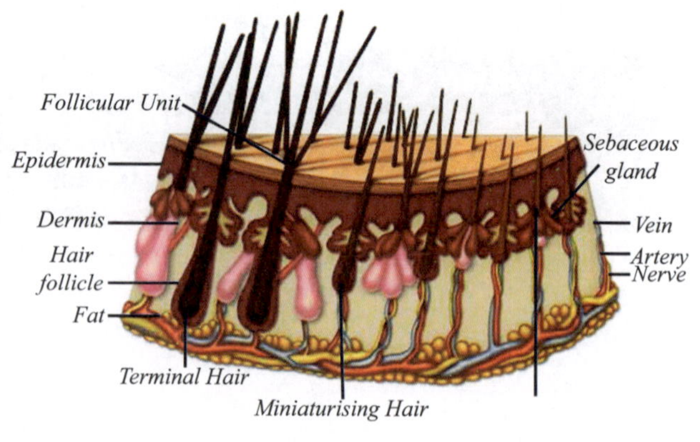

Hair Roots

to form the **keratin**. The root is inside a **follicle**, a small tube in the skin.

As the hair begins to grow, it pushes up from the root and comes out of the follicle, through the skin where it can be seen. The blood vessels present at the base of every follicle feed the hair root to nurture it. However, it is astonishing that once the hair is at the skin's surface, the cells within the strand of hair aren't alive anymore. The hair you see on every part of your body contains **dead cells**.

Nearly every hair follicle is attached to a **sebaceous gland**, which is also known as the *oil gland*. These produce oil, which makes the hair shiny.

You have more than *100,000 hairs on your head*, but you lose some every day. About 50 to 100 hairs fall out each day, while you're washing your hair, brushing or combing it, or just sitting still.

Hair Colour

The hair colour comes from a pigment called **melanin**. It is the substance that gives hair and skin its pigment. The lighter someone's hair, the less melanin there is. A person with brown or black hair has much more melanin than someone with blond or red hair. Some hair follicles are structured in a way that produces *curly hair*, whereas others send out *straight hair*. Follicles also determine if your hair will be *thick and coarse* or *thin and fine*.

Hair Care

With hair, the main thing is to keep it clean. Some people wash their hair every day, but others do it just once or twice a week. It depends on your hair and the kind of things you've been doing, like exercising or swimming.

Quick Facts

- Usually people will only notice that you are balding when you have lost almost 50 percent of the hair on your scalp. When you reach that stage, it might be too late to recover back all your hair.
- About 35 metres of hair fibre is produced every day on the average adult scalp.
- Hair is the fastest growing tissue in the body, second only to the bone marrow.
- Thyroid imbalance and iron deficiency are reversible causes for hair loss.
- Many drugs can also cause hair loss.
- About 90 percent of the scalp hair grow and 10 percent keep resting.
- The average scalp has 100,000 hairs. Redheads have the least at 80,000; brown and black haired persons have about 100,000; and blondes have the most at 120,000.
- The maximum length of the human hair is 70 to 90 cm.

- The female hair grows more slowly than the male hair.
- The lifespan of a human hair is 3 to 7 years on an average.
- Cutting the hair does not influence its growth.
- Wet hair should not be rubbed since hair is very sensitive.
- Generally, a hair strand's lifespan is five and a half years.
- Hair grows faster in summer than in winter and more in day than at night.
- We lose around 50 to 100 strands of hair each day.

Chapter - 9

THE FINGERNAILS

Fingernails are ideal for gripping objects and scratching itches. They are clear protective plates and prevent damage to the sensitive part of our upper fingertips.

Fingure Nails

Fingernails are produced by living skin cells in the finger. They consist of several parts, which include the *nail plate*, which is the visible part of the nail, the *nail bed*, which is the skin beneath the nail plate, the *cuticle*, which is the tissue that overlaps the plate and rims the base of the nail, the *nail folds*, which is the skin folds that frame and support the nail on three sides, the *lunula*, which is the whitish half-moon at the base of the nail and the *matrix*, which is the hidden part of the nail unit under the *cuticle*.

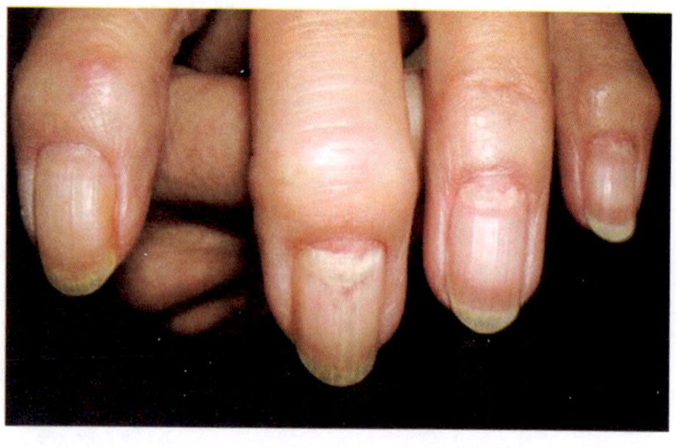

Fingernails grow from the matrix

Fingernails grow from the matrix. The nails are composed largely of *keratin*, which is a hardened protein and is also found in our skin and hair. As new cells grow in the matrix, the older cells are removed, compacted and take on the familiar flattened, hardened form of the fingernail. The cells that make nails die, flatten and fill with keratin as they are pushed forward from the nail's root.

Normal nail

Dry, brittle nail

It is interesting to know that the average growth rate for nails is 0.1 mm each day (or 1 centimetre in 100 days). However, the exact rate of nail growth depends on numerous factors, which include age and sex of individual and also the time of year. Fingernails generally grow faster in young people, in males, and in the summer.

It is another interesting fact that fingernails grow faster than toenails. The fingernails on the right hand of a right handed person grow faster than those on their left hand, and vice versa.

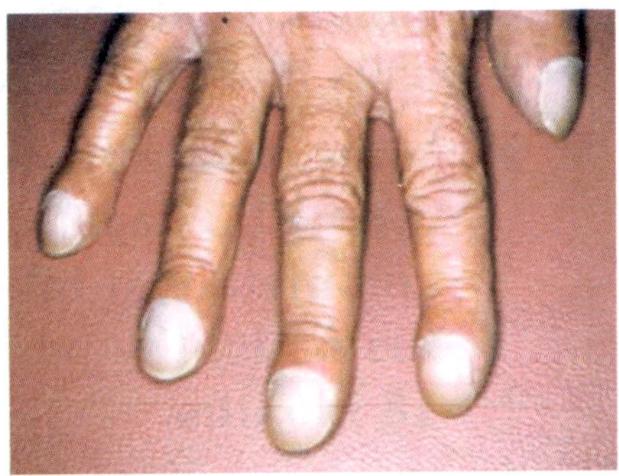

Brittle Nails

Our fingernails tell a lot about our body's health. Many of the body's deficiencies are reflected in our nails. For example, **brittle nails** reflect a *deficiency of calcium*, whereas **yellow nails** depict serious *liver problems*. **Blue nails** are a sign of **circulatory problem**.

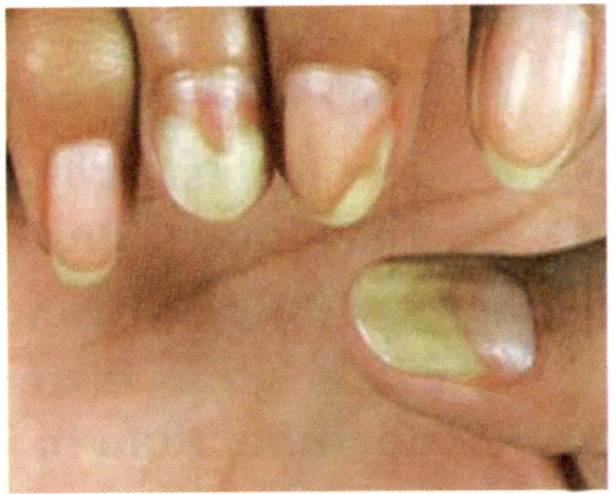

Yellow Nails

Hence, it is extremely important to keep a regular check on your overall health as it is evident that the entire body suffers due to problems that are concentrated in only one part.

Quick Facts

- About 1cm of nail takes 100 days to grow.
- Men's nails grow faster than a woman's nails.
- Nails are actually the same as hair. Both hair and nails are made of the same protein, called keratin.
- The nail plates are dead cells. However, the nail beds and the cuticles are live cells and they do need oxygen, vitamins and minerals.
- Nails don't sweat. The nail bed does not have sweat glands, so it can't perspire. It is the skin around the nails that gets sweaty.
- Nails grow at the rate of 0.1 mm daily (or 1 cm in every 100 days). So, for a finger nail to grow again completely, it takes between 4 and 6 months. For toe nails, the period of complete growth is 12 to 18 months.
- Finger nails for both genders grow faster than toe nails.
- Toe nails are about twice thicker than finger nails.
- The fastest growing nail is on the middle finger. The slowest on the thumbnail.
- Seasons and weather also affect the growth of nail. Nails grow faster in warm climates and during daytime, than in cold climates and at night.

Exercises

I. Answer the following questions.

1. How many organ systems are there in the human body?
2. What are basic constituents of the human body?
3. What is a cell and what are different kinds of cells present in a human body?
4. Describe briefly the following types of cells with diagrams:

   (i) Red Blood Cells(RBCs) (ii) White Blood Cells(WBCs)

   (iii) Nerve Cells
5. Where are the Epithelial Cells present and what are their functions?
6. Why is the human blood red in colour? What are the chief constituents of the blood?
7. Draw a diagram of the brain and label its different parts. Also, explain each part of the brain briefly with its functions.
8. How many sense organs do we have? Draw a diagram of each of them and explain them briefly.
9. Explain the Respiratory System in human beings with the help of a diagram.
10. Explain all about the Digestive System in human beings with the help of a diagram.

II. Fill in the blanks with suitable words.

1. The ________ filter and take the waste out of the blood, and make urine.
2. The length of the small intestine is about ____________ feet long.
3. Our ___________ can hold up to 1.5 litres of water or liquid material.
4. ___________ to and from the brain travel as fast as 170 miles per hour.
5. The size of the _______ is about the same size of a fist.
6. The heart is a very special kind of _______. Its job is to send blood all over the body.
7. The human heart is divided into four chambers. The upper two chambers are called as ___________ and the lower chambers are called _________.
8. A bundle of muscles extends from the floor of the mouth to form the ___________.
9. Nutrition can be broadly categorised into three types of food, such as: __________, ___________ and ___________.
10. __________ and _________ are part of the natural immunity system where the body is trying to eject pathogens and irritants from the respiratory system.

III. Match the two columns correctly.

A	B
1. If your saliva cannot dissolve something,	is present in our ears.
2. The smallest bone in the human body, called the stirrup	you cannot taste it.
3. We lose half a litre of water a day	206 bones.
4. The human body consists of	through breathing.

IV. Multiple Choice Questions (MCQs)

1. Hair is the fastest growing tissue in the body, second only to the ___________.

   a. Bone marrow. b. Blood. c. Fingernails. d. None of these

2. The fastest growing nail is on the middle finger. The slowest is the ___________.

   a. Ring finger. b. Little finger.

   c. Thumb nail. d. None of thess

3. Vitamin D is manufactured in the skin and is essential for ___________.

   a. digesting curd. b. digesting vegetables

   c. digesting milk. d. None of these

4. The buttock muscle is the ________ muscle of the body.

   a. smallest b. biggest c. medium d. None of these

5. The skeletal muscles form ________ of the body weight.

   a. 40 percent b. 50 percent

   c. 60 percent d. None of these

6. The first seven vertebrae at the top are called the ___________.

   a. thoracic vertebrae. b. cervical vertebrae.

   c. abdominal vertebrae. d. None of these

7. Humans have over _______ moveable and semi-moveable joints in their bodies.

   a. 250 b. 240

   c. 230 d. 260

8. After eating too much, your hearing becomes______ sharp.

   a. more b. less

   c. the same d. none of these

9. The backbone or the vertebral column consists of a long chain of _______bones, each individually known as a vertebra.

   a. 40 b. 33

   c. 48 d. 36

10. We breathe around __________of air each minute.

   a. 4.5 litres b. 5.5 litres

   c. 6.5 litres d. 8.5 litres

Glossary

Palate: The roof of the mouth

Pharynx: Throat

Uvula: Dangling flesh at the back of the mouth, contained in the soft palate

Tonsils: Clumps of tissue on both sides of the throat that help fight infections

Papillae: Tiny bumps on the tongue that contain the taste buds

Amylase: Digestive enzyme that starts the breakdown of carbohydrates even before food enters the stomach

Orbicularis oris: Major lip muscle that allows lips' mobility

Pulp: The innermost portion of teeth

Dentin: Hard, yellow substance which surrounds the pulp

Enamel: This forms the outermost layer of the crown, and protects the teeth

Cementum: A bony layer which covers the outside of the root and keeps the tooth in place

Cartilage: Soft and flexible material which is found in babies' bones

Bone Marrow: Soft, spongy material found at the centre of the bones; new blood cells are created here

Periosteum: Outer surface of the bones; contains nerve and blood cells

Compact bone: A layer next to the periosteum

Cancellous bone: A spongy layer within the compact bone

Sclera: The white part of the eyeball

Cornea: A transparent part which sits in front of the coloured part of the eye

Iris: The coloured part of the eye

Pupil: An opening through which light enters the eye

Anterior chamber: A space that is filled with a special fluid that keeps the eye healthy

Lens: The part of the eye that focuses the light rays to the retina

Retina: This changes the light rays into nerve signals and sends them to the brain

Vitreous: It is situated behind the retina and is the biggest part of the eye

Vitreous Humour: Clear, jelly-like material in the vitreous; light shines through this to the back of the eye

Rods and cones: These are used by the retina to process light

Lacrimal glands: These glands produce tears

Pinna or Auricle: The outer ear

Ossicles: Three, tiny bones in the ear, which help the sound in moving towards the inner ear

Cochlea: Small tube in the inner ear where sound waves are converted into nerve signals for the brain

Vertebral Column: Spine or backbone

Vertebrae/ Vertebra: A chain of ring-shaped bones in the spine

Cervical Vertebrae: The first seven vertebrae which support the head and neck

Thoracic Vertebrae: These hold the ribs of the chest primarily in place

Lumbar Vertebrae: The five vertebrae below the thoracic vertebrae

Sacrum: It is made of five vertebrae which are fused to form one single bone; situated below the lumbar

Coccyx: One bone made of the four fused vertebrae, below the sacrum

Cardiovascular System: The circulatory system which regulates the blood flow all over the body

Atria: The top or upper two chambers of the heart, which carry blood to the heart from different parts of the body and the lungs

Ventricles: The bottom or the lower two chambers of the heart. They carry blood from the heart to all parts of the body including the lungs

Septum: The thick wall of muscle which separates the left and right side of the heart

Mitral valve and Tricuspid valve: This allows the blood flow from the atria to the ventricles

Aortic valve and Pulmonary valve: They control the flow of the blood as it leaves the heart

Arteries: Blood vessels that carry blood away from the heart

Veins: They carry blood back to the heart

Pulse: Rhythmic expansion of arteries

Synovial fluid: This is a special fluid that helps the joints move freely

Ligaments: These make the bones hold on to the joints

Meninges: The layers of membranes which cushion the vertebrae

Central Nervous System (CNS): It receives information from the brain and sends information to the Peripheral Nervous System (PNS)

Peripheral Nervous System (PNS): Various nerves branching out from the spinal cord to the entire body

Cerebrospinal fluid: This helps to protect the nerve tissues, keep it healthy, and remove the waste products

Neurons: Tiny cells which relay information to each other to perform various functions

Sensory Neurons: They send information from the sensory receptors towards the Central Nervous System

Motor Neurons: They send information from the Central Nervous System to the muscles or glands

Sensory Nervous System: This sends information to the Central Nervous System (CNS) from our internal body organs or from the external stimuli

Motor Nervous System: It carries information from the CNS to different organs, muscles and glands

Somatic Nervous System: It controls the skeletal muscles as well as the external sensory organs, such as the eyes, nose, ears

Autonomic Nervous System: This controls the involuntary muscles, such as smooth and cardiac muscles

Sympathetic Nervous System: It controls activities that require high amounts of energy. It prepares the body for any kind of sudden stress or tension

Parasympathetic Nervous System: This controls activities that conserve the body's energy and help it to rest

Excretory System: This removes waste products from the body

Kidneys: They filter and take the waste out of the blood and make urine. These are the main organs of the excretory system

Ureters: These are the tubes that carry the urine to the bladder

Bladder: A bag that collects the urine

Urethra: A tube that carries the urine out of the body

Renal: Anything in the body related to the kidneys

Nephrons: Tiny filters which remove waste products

Homeostasis: It is the balance of the volume of fluids and minerals in the body done by the kidneys

Dialysis: People with malfunctioning kidneys often have to go through this process, where they are hooked up to a machine that filters their blood and acts as an artificial kidney